Praise for *Happy Endings*

"The book's most shocking aspect—aside from its placement at No. 4 on the *New York Times* best-seller list—is its sincerity. In addition to you-are-there depictions of sexual misadventure, Norton reveals much about his insecurities, his teenage rehab stint, bungled attempts at finding love and what goes on inside a mind that produces such hilarious outrageousness on a regular basis."

—*New York Post*

"Opie and Anthony resident loudmouth and stand-up comedian Jim Norton rants on-air against fatties, man boobs, sex with prostitutes. . . . No wonder he's so unbelievably popular. Norton has channeled his vitriolic humor into his new collection of essays."

—*Metro*

"Norton's first editorial offering is a realistic look at his rise from his parents' North Brunswick, NJ, basement and up the ranks of the cutthroat stand-up comedy circuit."

—*Mass Appeal*

JIM NORTON

I Hate Your Guts

SSE

SIMON SPOTLIGHT ENTERTAINMENT

New York London Toronto Sydney

SIMON SPOTLIGHT ENTERTAINMENT
A Division of Simon & Schuster, Inc.
1230 Avenue of the Americas
New York, NY 10020

First Simon Spotlight Entertainment hardcover edition November 2008

SIMON SPOTLIGHT ENTERTAINMENT and colophon are
trademarks of Simon & Schuster, Inc.

For information about special discounts for bulk purchases,
please contact Simon & Schuster Special Sales at
1-800-456-6798 or business@simonandschuster.com.

Manufactured in the United States of America

10   9   8   7   6   5   4   3   2   1

Library of Congress Cataloging-in-Publication Data is available.

ISBN-13: 978-1-4165-8785-9
ISBN-10:   1-4165-8785-3

This book is dedicated to anyone who sits in front of the television screaming *"Fuck you!"* for at least two hours a day.

Bad hair day . . . where did this shit come from? What a superficial culture. Put on a hat and go to work, you shallow cunt.

—GEORGE CARLIN, twentieth-century American poet

(917) 267-2602

This is a legitimate phone number. I listen to messages left here, and at times respond to them. It's not a scam; check it out on my MySpace page if you're skeptical (Myspace.com/jimnorton). Leave a message, tell me how much you loved the book. Or hated it. Or whatever else you want to tell me.

Contents

I Hate Your Guts

Preface

GEORGE CARLIN died yesterday and I'm goddamn depressed about it. He had a career that spanned fifty years and included fourteen HBO specials, so maybe I shouldn't be depressed about it. But I am. I'm sad and distracted and have been crying like a little fruit off and on for the last twenty-four hours.

Late last night I wanted to forget my troubles, so I figured I'd sit on the bowl and drop a few logs. For some people it's chanting *Nam Myoho Renge Kyo*, for me it's shitting. While perched on the toilet, the thought, *This is the first dump I've ever taken without George Carlin being on the earth* actually flashed through my mind, so I glanced around for a pistol to straighten myself out with. A marble-size nugget dropped into the water like a wedding ring. I pulled my pants up without flushing or wiping, and slinked into bed. And tonight is no better. I just feel . . . off. Empty. I tried having sex, and opted out after three minutes because my cock had the stability of the Somalian parliament. Hard to explain to a woman how you'd love to fuck, but you just can't seem to get this cantankerous, seventy-one-year-old dead genius off your mind . . .

First Pryor, now Carlin. Their being gone somehow makes me feel older; more alone. Especially George, who had been actively performing and shooting specials almost right up until the day he died. To so many comics, he was kind of a creative and professional father figure. No matter what the current event was, he did a better job addressing it than the rest of us. As much as I loved him, he depressed me by showing the greatness a comic could achieve. He was a constant and prolific barometer and I was never going to quite measure up.

Watching him perform made it feel cheesy and unsatisfying to go onstage and tap dance for approval. He made me feel compelled to be honest, regardless of how the audience felt about my opinions. And he was omnipresent, because whenever you felt lazy or complacent about diving into new material—hovering there, shaming you, was Carlin. And just when you thought you had him figured out morally, he'd turn and bite the throat out of whichever ideology he appeared to have his arm around the shoulder of.

Like or dislike him, agree or disagree with him, he was what all comedians dream of being when we start out; he was pure. He wasn't known as an actor, a personality, or a shitty humorist—he was a comic. A belligerent, taunting asshole of a comic. And he was beautiful. He'd go onstage, completely un-needy, never asking the audience for a goddamn thing, other than to remain attentive while he kicked them squarely in the balls. He attacked conservative and liberal institutions with equal harshness and disdain. And his attacks were visceral and precise. I think his greatest gift was his uncanny ability to reach into the guts of something and immediately expose the phony, embarrassing nature of its core. The one advantage to being a virtual nobody is that I never had to endure being deconstructed by him.

Many of the "cultural abominations" Carlin detested so much were being actively practiced by members of his audience. That never deterred him. In fact, it seemed to fuel him to drive the message home harder: *Since you're the people I'm talking about, here are the things you'll need to stop doing if you'd like me to stop attacking you. . . .* His almost sociopathic lack of begging, lack of asking the audience for one ounce of agreement, is something I'll never stop being in awe of. And it never felt like Carlin was out to shock or offend an audience; he was simply telling the truth. How they handled it was up to them.

Recently, George came into the studio, and I was able to interview/hang with him with Op & Ant. He stayed on for about forty minutes and talked about being old and dying. He also talked about how Islam is eventually going to win the religious war because they're relentless. In typical, brutally honest Carlin fashion, he pointed out that he'd probably be dead by then, but—and he smiled when he said this—many of us would still be alive to "feel the blade." We laughed, but it was also chilling in a way, because he obviously meant it.

The first time I met George was in January 1990 (three months before I ever set foot onstage myself), after taping his HBO special *Doin' It Again* at the State Theater in New Jersey. (If you watch the special, you can catch quick glances of my idiotic face about three rows back, center stage.) I wanted to meet him, so I blatantly lied to his road manager at the foot of the stage and told him I was a comedian. He looked around conspiratorially and sighed, ". . . Alright, come on," and brought my friend Gary and me backstage. It was my first time ever being "backstage" and I handled it with the same calm collectedness Travis Bickle displayed when mingling with Secret Service agents. There was a shitload of people there, and eventually Carlin wandered in and greeted everyone. I nervously introduced myself, so of course he made fun of my last name, mentioned he'd just quit drinking coffee, and signed my ticket. I told him I wanted to do stand-up, and he was friendly and encouraging, although I can't remember a fucking word he said. (Proving what a horse's ass I am. I had the rare opportunity to get comedy advice from George Carlin, and my brain decided that his quitting coffee was a more important fact to remember.)

The next time we met was almost fourteen years later, on the set of

Preface

Tough Crowd. In *Happy Endings*, I described the Act 3 sketch I did with Colin and George. They played priests and I was the altar boy who interrupted the scene to get a Carlin album signed. He called Colin and me cocksucking motherfuckers, which was not only funny, but behaviorally accurate. We also did Acts 1, 2, and 4 together. George and I sat on the couch (as it should have been, the two celebrities), and Nick DiPaolo and Greg Giraldo were across from us. What struck me that day was how we were all on our best behavior in front of Carlin. Typically, we would have been attacking each other, but not on that day. We all did our thing, but there was an unspoken reverence for George. An adoration. Whenever he started to speak, the four other big mouths on the panel slammed shut and waited for him. And it wasn't an issue of his fame. Other famous comics had been on, and at best had been interrupted, at worst had been yelled at.

Making George Carlin laugh; it's kind of like making Jenna Jameson cum. At least that's what I tell myself.

Preface

As much as I loved our third act together, it wasn't my favorite moment of the day. That happened earlier. Before the audience was seated, we got called down to the stage for rehearsal and blocking. (Carlin wanted no special treatment; he came down and went through the annoying camera blocking with the rest of us.) Afterward, when we were upstairs, I was walking by George's dressing room. As I passed his door, he called out, "Hey, Jim." I went into his dressing room, attempting to look casual. (I didn't feel casual. I wanted to kangaroo-hop down the hallway screaming, "George Carlin finally knows my name, you faggots!")

As I entered, he held up a bunch of 3x6 note cards, and asked me where I hid my notes on the set. Since I knew where he was sitting, I told him where he could hide his papers on the little table next to the couch without the camera seeing them. I guess what I loved so much about that moment was that a comedian of his magnitude cared enough about being funny on the show to have notes prepared. He didn't take the laughs for granted. More important, I loved that he was the same neurotic schmuck that I was about hiding them on the set. And of course, that when he needed to know where to hide them, he saw me walking by, and thought, *Jim's a comic, I'll ask him.* At least that's how I chose to see it. He very well may have asked the first two-legged creature he saw, which just happened to be me. Am I creating a "comedian bonding moment" out of a random question that had nothing to do with me as a comic and everything to do with me waltzing by an open door as he thought of it? Probably.

I think Carlin would've liked this book, and I don't mean the writing or the jokes. He may have found my writing poorly thought-out and primitive. Or even worse, mediocre and boring. But I know he'd have enjoyed where it came from. It's uncomfortably honest. And parts of it are uncomfortably brutal. And needless to say, parts of it are uncomfortably maudlin (see beginning of page one up to the beginning of this sentence). There are people I loathe and I wrote a book shitting all over them; the concept of that would have pleased him. The honesty of it. Not the subjective right or wrong of it, but the fact that I'm telling the truth. And I think it's funny. At least, I hope it is. Because, in the end, my job isn't to preach to you, or to change your opinion about anything, but to make you laugh. If I make you think but not laugh, then I've failed miserably and should stand around the watercooler and brag about being the smartest cunt in the office. If I do neither, then I should just stand around the same watercooler with my fucking mouth shut.

Depressingly, I'll never get Carlin's take on my book—good, bad, or indifferent, because he's as dead as a fucking doornail (or, as mother used to say, he went "bye-bye in a box"). Which is sad. And also kind of scary. Because it means, by default, that we're all one step closer to feeling the blade. Good-bye, George, and thanks for everything, we loved you.

Heather Mills:
I Am Woman, Hear Me Hop

I THINK Paul McCartney has lost his fucking mind. It's the only explanation I can come up with as to why he not only would marry a one-legged woman in her thirties, but also knock her up and then divorce her without a prenup. What a complete and utter idiot. This is the equivalent of putting an oscillating fan in front of a giant pussy and throwing $1.5 billion into it. How good of a bang was she, for Pete's sake? When he licked her twat did it open up and sing "Band on the Run"? Or maybe it was the stump that got him; I hear he used to put a fedora on it and pretend it was Jack Ruby. Whatever it was, something about their sex took an otherwise brilliant man and turned his brain into mush (which supports my theory that she was also fucking George Harrison).

If a woman is good in bed, and I mean really good in bed (not just perfunctory moves like winking while she's giving head or queefing the national anthem), there is virtually no limit to what she can motivate a man to do. And I don't want to hear that he loved her; I've seen her interviewed, and she has the personality of the Queen's asshole. She absolutely sucks. But, she is undeniably sexy. There is something about that accent, combined with the rumors that she used to be a high-priced load receptacle, that makes her appealing.

The former secretary of arms dealer (wrong limb, Heather, wrong limb!) Adnan Khashoggi claimed that he paid thousands to sleep with her, and that she was "very athletic" in bed. (Maybe he liked his big Arab balls juggled by a gal who could dismount parallel bars and land with her brown eye directly on his nose.) If she really was an international hooker, it certainly explains why dumb Paul displayed financial Down syndrome. I'm sure Linda was a terrific gal, but there's no way she could've competed in the sack with a girl who fucked swarthy billionaires for a living.

Reading accusations that Heather used to be a whore actually made me want to meet up with her to try to work a little something out. I'd love to pinch and squeeze my hog through my khakis while haggling prices with her: "All right, you drive a hard bargain, but here's what I'll do. You get five hundred if you leave the leg on, or a dollar fifty if you insist on taking it off . . . minus the cost of fumigating the room. You get another hundred if you let me stick it in your ass, a hundred and fifty if you're bent over wearing a flamingo outfit. And just to show you that I'm not a hard-hearted man, that it's not all dollars and cents, you get fifty more if I accidentally cum in your hair, and an extra fiver if you hop around the room screaming, 'I'm a cunt!' while holding the fake leg against your forehead like a rhinoceros." Negotiations like that would have undoubtedly been good-natured and fun, while sending her the message that my finances would be doled out generously, but not up for grabs. Apparently McCartney was old-school, and not comfortable tossing her a few hundred just to lick his balls while he jerked off in the Bentley.

Heather told *Vanity Fair* that she offered to sign a prenup so that he would know she loved him for him, and that Sir Lovestruck turned her down (thereby justifying my opening line in the first paragraph). This is the most blatant case of reverse psychology I have ever read, and to fall for it one would have to be completely retarded or completely enthralled by a vagina that's a quarter-century younger than oneself. So for any woman who really doesn't want to sign a prenup, don't fight it—suggest it! Bring it up aggressively and the pussy-whipped *dope* you are engaged to will shake his fist and shout, "Stop with all of this prenuptial agreement malarkey, I won't hear of it!"

In the same article she admitted that their favorite thing to do was stay home, where she would cook a meal and he would dance around the room like Fred Astaire. She claimed that watching him like that made her want to eat him up. My heart sunk when I read that. You poor doddering, knighted idiot: Did you really think she would peek out into the living room and dampen her panties watching an old man sashay around like Fred Astaire? She probably loved seeing you dance like that because it implied senility, thereby making it easier to bilk you out of everything.

In the end, I heard she got almost forty-nine million dollars for four years' work, which was over two hundred million less than she asked for. (I've heard so many different figures. Except for the one she should have gotten, which is a fat fucking goose egg.) Not bad. If life was fair, she would have left that marriage with a *Beatles Anthology* and a bag of pristine left shoes. So much for liking him just for him, huh? Greedy cunt.

The more I've read about their marriage, the more I despise her. I think she took a very well-oiled pussy and used it to rake a great artist over the coals. I have no idea if her allegations of him abusing her are true, although if they're not, they should be. At the risk of sound sexist, when you marry a gentleman who has more than a billion in the bank, an occasional fist to the jaw should not only be taken in stride, it should be expected and welcomed with a smile. Don't be such a tattletale for Christ's sake. Perhaps I'm exposing myself here, but when I read some of her allegations, I cheered loudly for Sir Paul the Batterer. Looking around online, these are a few of the allegations I found against him:

- Heather actually had the audacity to complain that Paul wanted her to make dinner every night. Churlish twat— she should have hummed a Fred Astaire song and tongued his taint while he ate rice pudding out of her shitty prosthetic. Her whole job in that situation was to keep the breadwinner happy.

- That he pushed her violently when she was pregnant. He probably did the math and realized what another kid would cost him, so he figured a miscarriage would be the equivalent of an eighteen-year tax deferment. Violently shoving a woman when she's pregnant is a bad move, as it is nearly impossible to justify legally. In cases where a linebacker-esque shoulder to the midsection is called for, try the "old whoops-a-daisy" instead. The "old whoops-a-daisy" is achieved when one sticks one's foot out at the top of the stairs, causing the knocked-up gold digger in question to take a Three Stooges tumble down the stairs. While watching the tumble, said gentleman must retract his guilty foot while remarking, "Whoops-a-daisy!" loud enough to be overheard.

- Paul asked her not to breast-feed because he claimed that "they were his breasts" and that he "didn't want a mouth full of breast milk." Bravo! No man in his right mind wants to invest almost a billion dollars in a pair of tits that are going to resemble leaky saddlebags in a year. You're already minus half a leg, now you want to dump your tits down the chute as well? Maybe you should also have your pussy sewn shut, and Sir Paul could just lay you on your side and dry hump your armpits every now and again.

- Paul drank a lot and used drugs, despite promising not to. How could this phony bitch claim to be surprised or outraged? Did she actually think "Yellow Submarine" was about four 1960s junkies taking a homoerotic, underwater boat ride? Or that "Lucy in the Sky with Diamonds" was written in honor of a flying, bedazzled hosebag? Wake up, stupid. He was at the forefront of the biggest drug culture in history; consider yourself lucky he didn't force you to use that plastic appendage to mule prescription drugs or Ecstasy.

- He forced her to postpone a crucial operation because it interfered with his Amsterdam vacation plans. Good for him. This makes me want to marry a woman who needs a crucial operation, just so I can tell her to toughen the fuck up while I window-shop for Dutch prostitutes (even more effective if you've possibly married a British one).

- And my personal favorite: he objected to her using a bedpan. According to Heather, the bedpan saved her the trouble of crawling to the toilet at night. She couldn't understand why he objected. Gee, I don't know, maybe because he wrote "Yesterday"? Maybe that kind of entitles him to live out his life not waking up with a shit and piss medley staring at him eye level from a pan on the nightstand. And I think "crawling" to the bathroom is just a bit melodramatic:

How about you leave a crutch by the bed, drama queen? I didn't realize that without the G.I. Joe leg you were reduced to crawling, yet with it you feel comfortable enough to dance on national television (or more accurately, fall on national television). I'm surprised that when your tailbone hit the floor some of Paul's money didn't shoot out of your cunt. And that really was the only reason to watch you on that shitty show; I wanted to see the bad leg fall off or the good one break.

One of the greatest things I've ever read revolved around this idiot and her stupid dancing phase. Heather and her *Dancing with the Stars* partner were on a very delayed flight from L.A. to London and all of the passengers were bored and cranky. The captain made an apologetic announcement and said he had a nice surprise for the passengers to make up for their nightmare trip. After some flapping and commotion behind the first-class curtain, it ripped open and this absolute asshole and her partner *did a tango down the fucking aisle*. Doesn't that just make you want to shit on a plate and eat it? A tango. And then the best part: they finish their dance with a flourish and . . . NOTHING! No applause, no accolades, no nothing. Just her in summery white pants and the sound of jet engines. I would have killed to have been there, as I feel a well-placed "Booooo" would have galvanized the other passengers into a mutiny.

How completely out of touch she must be not to realize that every person on that plane thinks she's dogshit personified and would have felt more entertained if Muhammad Atta had popped out from behind the curtain. And having the captain make an apology over the loudspeaker was a terrible idea because everyone probably thought they were getting a free flight. Nope, no free flight here, folks—just the most hated woman in Europe and her fruity friend doing an out-of-date dance, and to top it off, she doesn't even have the decency to fall at the end of it for your amusement.

And I'm sick of hearing about the charities she's associated with; I'm not impressed. Even her charity work seems self-centered. One of the things she campaigns against are land mines, which I think is hilarious. Worried about losing the other one, aren't you, shithead? Next she'll be campaigning against trip wires, deep holes, and bear traps. She and Sir Pussy-Whipped belonged to the Adopt-a-Minefield program. I'd love to join this program, just to build a fence around my minefield and let kids play in it.

Heather's also big on animal causes, one of which is pig welfare. How appropriate. Pig Welfare should be the program she's forced to join in order to collect McCartney's money. Either that, or PETA should allow her to campaign only on behalf of kangaroos, rabbits, frogs, and grass-hoppers. There was one lovely moment in her animal campaign history—when she went to deliver a PETA DVD to J. Lo and her bum leg came off. Originally it was reported that it came off in a scuffle, until Heather came out and explained what really happened. She said that her leg "got hot and came off because of the heat." Ewwwww. How awful does sweaty stump smell? And what the hell is it made out of, ceramic? Try a little Krazy Glue, you dizzy bitch.

Although I detest Heather Mills, I don't totally fault her. No one held a gun to Stupid's head and forced him to marry her. And I'm sure his lawyers and definitely his kids were screaming when he decided not to go with a prenup. And then the atomic bomb: she had a baby. When that kind of money is at stake, you should only stick your dick in ears, mouths, and belly buttons. Protecting that cash should always be in the forefront of your mind. I wouldn't even have anal sex with her for fear that after I came she'd sneeze and some would leak down into her pussy and mosey on up to her womb. Then for the next eighteen years, I'd be forking over income for a load that just as easily could have wound up in a sock.

YOU WANT EVERYONE TO STOP HATING YOU, HEATHER? HERE'S A LITTLE FREE ADVICE . . .

- Call a press conference and offer to reconcile with Stella McCartney by eating her pussy.
- Go on a seal hunt and giggle like a schoolgirl as you club their fat little bodies.
- Always wear a black prosthetic leg with a miniskirt; it's hard for me to hate someone who makes me laugh.
- Suck my dick. As hard as it is for me to hate you once you make me laugh, once I cum in your mouth, I'm putty in your hands.
- Tango on another transatlantic flight and finish the dance with a flourish by flinging open your arms as you body-check yourself into the emergency exit door handle.
- Star in a homemade porno where you're being fucked doggy style and the guy has your left side propped up with phone books.
- While enjoying a Tanzanian safari, get your fake leg stuck in the mud as a baboon is attacking you.

Little Jimmy Norton, the Prettiest Girl on the Team

MY LOVE for the Yankees was the only thing that could have motivated me to play a sport. Of all the sports, baseball was the only one I ever tried (unless you consider it a sport to kneel by the side of your bed and hold your shits in for so long it causes stomach cramps, in which case I'm a Hall of Famer). I certainly wasn't destined to be one of the greats. I think I was a fourth grader my first year in Little League, and I played right field for Young's Glass Service. Ah, yes, the dream of every boy: to play for a team named after a storm window installation company. Quite an accomplishment, second only to playing shortstop for Marv's Plaque Removal or being the backup catcher for the East Brunswick Rape Crisis Center.

To be honest, I sucked ass and was lucky to get any playing time at all. Although I wore number 3 like Babe Ruth, I got two hits all season like Ruth Gordon. And I was virtually worthless in the outfield. To say I played right field wasn't entirely true; I played between center and right field (this is a special position in the outfield, created for kids in wheelchairs). This told everyone that there were only ten square feet in the outfield the coaches felt I could cover effectively.

Throughout my life, I've been plagued with the occasional twitch or nervous habit. In fourth grade, I had a particularly heinous one: I would, on occasion, spin in a complete circle to my right. There was no rhyme or reason, but there were times when it just needed to be done. And it wouldn't be a flamboyant *swirl!* ending in a flourish—just a slow, regular spin—and always to the right. (All good boys and girls spin to the right; spinning once to the left is the sign of the Jew: John 14:2.) Having a twitch of this sort is unobtrusive when being acted out in one's room. However, it's slightly more conspicuous when being performed in the outfield of a Little League game.

One particular afternoon we were getting the living shit kicked out of us by Burger King (on the surface this makes us sound like a bunch of queers. But I'll have you know that Burger King won the championship that year. They played the Autism Society of America and won a real nail-biter, 147–0.) So we're being routed and I'm standing in the outfield kind of zoning out with my thumb and pointer finger up my nose making the roly-poly motion. Without warning, my central nervous system determines it's time for a full circle spin, and I willingly oblige. A few minutes pass and wouldn't you know it—I'm nervous again. What if a ball gets hit to me and I drop it?? I'm so nervous I don't know what to do . . . wait a minute, I have it. I know exactly what I'll do! I'll spin in a circle to the right again! And I did. I went through this ritual about four times, oblivious to the fact that I was in full view of my team, Burger King, and all of our coaches and families. Just a boy, slight of build, wearing Babe Ruth's number and spinning in circles.

All of a sudden, from the other side of the field on the bench, I hear my coach bellow, "Hey, Jimmy, what are you, a ballerina??" As quiet as it was, he could have whispered it and everyone would have heard it. But he didn't whisper it; he screamed it like James Cagney at the end of *White Heat*. I couldn't have heard it more clearly if he were kneeling on my shoulder with his balls resting on my head, crooning it into a bullhorn. I was fucking mortified. Complete, total, and instant humiliation.

Every man, woman, and child craned their necks to get a gander at the pretty dancing girl in almost-right field. Where is she, they wondered? Where is this magical fairy with a boy's name, pirouetting like it's the Christmas Eve performance of *The Nutcracker*? As they all stared dumbly at me, I decided to act like I didn't know this "Jimmy" faggot either. I punched the inside of my glove then did the put-my-hands-on-my-knees-and-lean-forward pose that baseball players are known for. I stared blankly ahead, a testament to the fact that a mistake had been

Young's Glass Service team photo. I am the creepy waif kneeling in the middle, squinting like the outlaw Josey Wales, with his hands folded psychotically on his knee. The coach on the left, with the glasses, was Mr. Wassenda. It was he who inquired loudly about my river dancing.

made, and there were in fact no toe-tapping poofters here in the outfield, just us boys who love baseball.

Keeping my mouth shut is the one thing I give myself credit for in hindsight. My first instinct was to actually answer him by yelling back, "No," as if it were meant to be a genuine question that he had been pondering. As if he and the coaches and other players and our families in the bleachers had discussed it and come to the conclusion that I must indeed be a dance prodigy. Upon hearing my response, they would just let it go and logically assume there must be a perfectly masculine explanation as to why I was alternately playing defense and spinning like a whirligig. I don't remember anything about that game, although if life were fair I'd have spent the rest of the season relegated to helping the equipment coach by carrying all of the bats in my asshole.

The following year was a bit better. I played for the Royals (although we were sponsored by Rutgers Wine & Liquor). It certainly wasn't a lot better, my hitting and fielding still sucked a dick, but at least I was smart enough to leave my ballet slippers in my knapsack. This was also my first year of wearing glasses, which did nothing but make my face look irresistibly punchable. I was again sent to right field as soon as my coaches realized my shitty depth perception made it hard for me to tell if a ball was a dribbler behind the plate or missiling toward the center of my face at 200 miles an hour.

My outfield skills were woefully lacking because not only could I not catch but, due to an offhanded compliment given to me by my Aunt Nancy, I also thought I had a much better arm than I did. (We were having a catch in the front yard of my grandmother's house when my dad approached us. Aunt Nancy remarked, "Boy, Jimmy's got an arm like a firecracker," and I beamed with pride as I wound up and whizzed the ball back up over her head and onto the roof, effectively ruining the moment.

I should've realized I misunderstood her when she tried to insert my arm into a frog's asshole.) At crucial moments in the game, I would constantly overthrow the cutoff man and underthrow the infielder, so the ball would land impotently on the grass in between them while the hitter moon-walked around the bases for an inside-the-park home run.

I did have one overtly humiliating experience; only this one occurred at the plate and left my sexuality out of it. It was my third time up, there were two outs, and I was 0 for 2, having been struck out badly twice. As soon as I settled into the batter's box, the outfielders began to slowly walk in—implying that it was my destiny to swing at and miss every pitch by at least four feet. Well, what do you know? The first pitch he throws at me I take a vicious cut and actually connect. The crack of the bat was unmistakable; I hit it! I quickly scanned to see where it was (flying deep into the outfield, or was it a line drive over the shortstop's head?), and then glanced down at the first base foul line and saw it dying a slow death three feet away in foul territory. I've had precum leak out with more force.

My coaches and teammates were pressed up against the fence screaming, "Run! Run to first!" They even motioned toward first base frantically just in case I was having a stroke and had lost my sense of direction. There was no way I was running because the ball was foul and it would be embarrassing to run to first when the ball had traveled less than a yard. I stood there like a statue of Douche the Conqueror and watched the ball mockingly roll back into fair territory. As the pitcher casually leaned down and scooped it up, I dropped my bat and took off like a glacier, getting about two feet before he tossed it to first. My coaches and teammates just stared at me through the fence like I was the most useless, nonrunning cocksucker they'd ever seen. You'd think with my king-of-the-nerds glasses I'd have picked up the trajectory of the ball sooner.

See if you can pick me out. I'll give you a hint: think "bespectacled Chinese boy who looks like he should be accepting a gold medal in the Special Olympics."

My third year of Little League also found me playing for the Royals. Rumor had it they were trying to trade me to the Brewers for a dildo made of liverwurst, but the deal fell through when I failed the physical. This was also the first season I talked about pitching. I guess I wasn't ready to let my Aunt Nancy's "firecracker arm" compliment die quite yet, so I started tossing to the catcher from the pitcher's mound and surprisingly, I was very accurate. We had a fairly good team that year; we were actually winning most of our games. One afternoon I was called in from the outfield to pitch in relief. I think there was one out, and I mowed down the next two batters with ease. Finally, I'd found my calling! I could pitch. After my debut in relief, the coaches decided I should start a game. No reason to let such talent wither and die in the outfield. All week I took pitching practice, throwing every day from the mound. I guess I was a bit nervous, which would explain why my control wasn't quite as good as it had been that day when I was called in with no time to think.

Saturday afternoon finally rolled around and I was shitting a brick. The sudden star of the bullpen was completely petrified. I wasn't used to being "the man" or the focus of all of this positive attention. How I yearned for the pressure-free days of standing in the outfield, wearing a tutu and doing battement tendu exercises. Taking my warm-up pitches before the game I was having more trouble finding the plate than Karen Carpenter. I tried to keep a stoic look on my face, praying my opponents would think it was par for the course that I hurled the ball over the catcher's head during warm-ups.

As the first batter approached the plate, my coach walked out and handed me the ball and told me to relax, just do what I do naturally. Let my ability take over. I smiled cockily and winked at him, "Not a problem, coach." What I really wanted to do was jump into his arms and beg him to take me home. I had so much sweat trickling down my back that the crack of my ass felt like Lake Gitchy Goomy. The first pitch was called a ball because it was just outside. And by "just outside" I mean the catcher reached as far as he could to his left and it still flew past his glove and smashed into the backstop. Next pitch went right over the middle of the plate. Unfortunately, it bounced in the dirt before it went over the plate, so I was down 2–0. Ball three followed immediately after, and the next pitch missed by so much the umpire didn't even say, "Ball four." It was going to be a real shit heap of an afternoon.

Batter two stepped up and I threw what would have been a called strike had home plate been two feet back and to the left. Behind me, I could hear my teammates trying to encourage me with chants of, "Nobatter-nobatter-nobatter," as I fired a fastball directly over the heart of the plate. Well, as luck would have it, this cocksucker was guessing fastball and drilled a double off the wall. (I say he was "guessing fastball" as if I had an arsenal to choose from. There were only two pitches for him to choose from: fastball that could be hit, or fastball that was so far outside the strike zone you'd need a rowing oar to make contact.) I now had runners on second and third, no outs, and the only strike I had thrown was belted like Marilyn Monroe after DiMaggio drank a pot of Mr. Coffee. I almost wanted to turn around and blame the infield, since they had assured me he was a nobatter-nobatter-nobatter, when he was in fact quite the batsman.

Naturally, I was now a bit gun-shy about tossing a strike, so I promptly walked the next batter on five pitches. It should have been four pitches, but the umpire called a mercy strike on a pitch that was only nine inches outside the strike zone. The other team had so little respect for me, the batter didn't even argue what was obviously a horrible call. He correctly assumed the next pitch would be a far-off-the-plate glop of shit. I glanced over the bench and my coach was on his knees with his head buried in his hands, openly weeping. I sensed his confidence in me was waning.

To make a long story short, the first nine batters reached base (seven walks, one hit, and one hit batsman). The coach only left me in that long because he was hoping a drunk driver would barrel onto the field and plow into me, saving him the embarrassment of having to walk out to the mound. I left with a 6–0 deficit, the bases loaded, and no outs. We got creamed. And my pitching on the team was never mentioned again. Not negatively, not positively. Just not mentioned. Kind of like a molestation, without the admirable notion of declaring your bloody asshole a war wound.

That third season had a sort of bittersweet ending. We wound up going to the championship game, which no one expected. We then proceeded to get our dicks kicked in, which everyone expected. It was the last inning and we were losing 13–1. There was a runner on first and one out. I swung hard at the first two pitches, creating a lovely breeze for any insects that happened to be fluttering about. The coaches signaled for the guy on first to steal, which is a wonderful statement about how shitty they felt I was. I am down two strikes and they run the guy on base, assuming that even if I do hit it, I'll ground into a double play. Well, I didn't. Breaking new ground at this point seemed silly, so I flailed the bat like I had Parkinsons once again and struck out. And the runner was thrown out. Double play, game over.

Ten-hut! You wouldn't hit a mongoloid with glasses, would ya?

EPILOGUE

I played for the Red Sox the following year and was an average hitter, but for some reason I remember none of the season at all. My only memory is of Barry, a black teammate of mine, telling my dad that I was one of the better hitters on the team. My father was very proud and relayed the compliment to me. I screamed at my father for believing anything said to him by a black kid named after one of the Bee Gees, and called him a you-know-what lover.

Reverend Al Sharpton, Scumbag Extraordinaire

IF YOU'RE white in America, it's almost racially mandatory that you hate this rancid windbag. He irritates white people so much, it's a gift you almost have to admire. He used to be much fatter, which was helpful in formulating his two-word nickname. The first word was "fat," and the second word would land me a great gig on *Seinfeld*.

For years we have been subjected to this loudmouth asshole trumpeting black victimhood on the nightly news. I've never seen his shitty fat face and Fred Flintstone hairdo without a microphone in front of him and the cast of *Moesha* loitering behind him. And it's always, without fail, about white people doing bad things to black people. Not once have I ever seen this verbose turd address black-on-white or black-on-black crime. I've provided a brief list of his greatest hits:

- **THE SUBWAY VIGILANTE, 1984.** On December 22, 1984, mild-mannered nerd/psychopath Bernhard Goetz sat on the No. 2 train, when four black teenagers surrounded him. One of them demanded five dollars, presumably to buy a new Trapper Keeper for college. While reaching into his wallet to help these enterprising young gentleman in their business venture, he accidentally pulled out a .38 Special and shot all four of them. The case was, of course, divided down racial lines. Sharpton and the rest of the vermin he associated with claimed that Goetz's actions were racist. The fact that Goetz had been mugged twice already in New York, once violently, didn't seem to persuade Reverend Sweatsuit otherwise. He also seemed to overlook the racial angle of Bernard looking like an easy target because he was a white dweeb who was so meek he made Bill Gates look like Charlie Bronson. Al demanded two federal civil rights investigations, and of course both of them concluded that the shootings were a result of an attempted rob-

A relaxed, warm moment with Bernhard Goetz—a take-no-guff citizen who really took a bite out of crime (well, four bites to be exact).

bery and not race. All four men survived, although Darrell Cabey was paralyzed as a result. He's been on his best behavior ever since.

- **HOWARD BEACH, 1986.** Three black men were chased out of Howard Beach, Queens, by a gang of white residents. One of them, Michael Griffith, was hit by a car and killed while trying to get away. Personally, I fault the driver of the car who hit him, because when driving by Howard Beach you should always be on the lookout for black men running for their lives.

- **TAWANA BRAWLEY CASE, 1987.** Fifteen-year-old Tawana Brawley was found outdoors, lying in a garbage bag with her clothes torn and racial slurs written in shit on her chest. (Initially, the police thought it was me after an expensive all-nighter with a dominatrix.) Brawley claimed to have been raped by six white men. Stupid Sharpton teamed up with two vomitous attorneys, Alton Maddox and C. Vernon Mason, to support this lying bitch.

  From the beginning, it was fairly obvious she was lying through her teeth (I just had to physically restrain myself from typing that she was "full of shit") because of inconsistencies in her story, like claiming one of the rapists was Tom Bosley, who not only raped her but provided the GLAD bag she was found in. She also had no injuries other than a small bruise behind her left ear. Six men assault you with their dicks and all you have is a bruise behind your ear? Tawana should have upped the believability factor by claiming they were Asian.

- **YUSEF HAWKINS MURDER, 1989.** For once Sharpton was in the right, protesting against a mob who attacked and shot this unarmed teenager. While marching through Bensonhurst, white counterprotesters were screaming "Nigger" and holding watermelons out in front of them. Since it is Brooklyn, I can't be sure if these were gestures of anger, or if residents actually considered these acts warm and welcoming. While preparing to lead a protest in January 1991, Sharpton was stabbed in the chest by a drunk attacker, Michael Riccardi. The jury failed to believe Mr. Riccardi's excuse that he slipped while attempting to cut the Reverend's meatball sub in half for him.

Michael Riccardi in 2008. One thing is for certain: the man has exquisite taste in reading material.

I Hate Your Guts

- **CROWN HEIGHTS RIOT, 1991.** A station wagon driven by a Hassidic Jew struck another car in an intersection, which caused him to veer onto the sidewalk and plow into a group of black children, killing one of them. A mob gathered and began beating him after he jumped out of his car and shouted, "Better call Geico!" Reverend Fat Douchebag organizes a peaceful protest, which of course turns into a four-day riot. Residents mourn the tragic death by beating up Jews and looting stores. (I guess nothing gets you over the death of a seven-year-old boy like a new pair of Jordans and a flat screen.)

  Visiting student Yankel Rosenbaum (winner of the Most Jewish Name in History award) was stabbed to death by a member of a mob screaming, "Kill the Jew!" Sharpton calmed tensions by stating, "If the Jews want to get it on, tell them to pin their yarmulkes back and come over to my house!" The Jews, having no grasp of urban slang, showed up at Sharpton's house in lingerie because they thought he was hitting on them. Mayor David Dinkins tried to stop the march, but had to abandon his efforts when Jessica Tandy demanded a ride to Piggly Wiggly.

- **FREDDIE'S FASHION MART, 1995.** Yet another case where Shitdick Al has a major confrontation with the Jews (you know, the terrible, awful Jews who've always been actively involved in such atrocities as the NAACP and civil rights movement). In this latest case of White Devil vs. Blameless People of Color, a Jewish landlord in Harlem was going to evict a black-owned business, the Record Shack.

Of course, there was a protest, where Sharpton uttered his famous, "We will not stand by and allow them to move this brother so that some white interloper can expand his business."

First of all, if Sharpton wanted that brother to stay put, he should have sat on him, making the brother too heavy to be moved by anyone. Second, if anyone's an interloper here, it's black people. Apparently, no one is brave enough to mention the early 1600s, when white settlers were minding their own beeswax, relaxing on land generously donated by the Indians. They then went over to Africa to be friendly and say hello. Africans stole their ships, then came to America to voluntarily help out with the chores. So Sharpton using this term is not only silly, but also easily confused with "white antelopers" (Harlem-dwelling Caucasians with horns and small, cloven hooves who avoid muggers by gracefully pronking to safety).

As what I believe to be a direct result of Fatso's racist speech, one of the protesters went into the store with a gun and flammable liquid. He shot customers, set the store on fire (killing seven employees via smoke inhalation), shot himself to death, and then stole a Public Enemy CD.

- **AMADOU DIALLO SHOOTING, 1999.** Unarmed immigrant Amadou Diallo was shot forty-one times and killed by police outside his building in the Bronx. Cops claimed the whole thing was a misunderstanding, but had a hard time explaining why they were yelling "Eenie meenie miny moe" as they fired. The officers thought he was drawing a gun, but it turned out to be a wallet. Once you realize you've pumped forty-one bullets into a guy who only had a wallet, I imagine it's one of those "I could've had a V8!" moments. Under cross-examination, the officers acknowledged they found it odd that his gun only seemed to be firing business cards and an expired learner's permit.

The case went to trial, and the officers were cleared of criminal wrongdoing, but forced to take shooting lessons to improve their abysmal aim. His family was eventually awarded $3 million by a jury, so it all worked out. This makes me want to have a kid just in hopes that he catches some lead and I can cash in.

- **UNDERCOVER FBI TAPE, 2002.** Almost twenty years after it happened, a video surfaced of Sharpton discussing a major cocaine buy with an undercover FBI agent. The tape was made sometime in 1983, and Reverend Tex looks utterly ridiculous with his unlit cigar and cowboy hat. The hat itself would have been fine if Al wasn't obese with a bouffant hairdo. He looked like three different Halloween costumes all being worn at the same time.

  The informant is talking about giving this thieving fuck a possible $35,000 commission to set up a coke buy. Sharpton claims that he didn't agree, and was only playing along because he thought Alan Funt would be walking out at any moment. He tried to sue HBO for airing the tape because it damaged his reputation by portraying him as a fat, drug-dealing slug with a hat like John Wayne and hair like Annette Funicello. HBO eventually settled out of court, agreeing to only shoot one season of *Lucky Louie* if Sharpton dropped his suit.

Imus trying to get high from licking a toad.

- **DON IMUS AND THE NAPPY-HEADED HOS,
  2007.** This is the case that makes me hate Reverend Shit for
  Brains more than all of the other ones combined. Everyone
  reading this remembers the incident, so I won't go over it
  moment by moment. But suffice to say it makes me want
  to grow my pubic hair back in just so I can yank it out in
  frustration.

  First of all, the nappy-headed hos joke was funny. I
  laughed at it, and anyone who was offended by it can go
  jump in the lake. The phony outrage manufactured by
  black people over this horseshit joke would be laughable if
  it didn't actually cost Imus his job. The same people who
  were "offended" would never, and I mean NEVER, try to

have a black personality yanked off the air for the same joke. Black people have become irritatingly hypersensitive, while white people have become groveling, unabashed faggots. It wasn't surprising when Reverend White Interlopers had to get his bulldoggish jowls into the mix. That fat fucking attention whore.

Imus made a stupid mistake when he went on Sharpton's show because it kept the story going. He never should have walked into such a hostile atmosphere and expected a fair shot; apparently he's never seen *Black Hawk Down*. Sharpton then resorts to using visual aids by bringing his daughter out as though that's supposed to have an emotional impact and drive the point home. Imus should have told him to go fuck himself, and then asked the magically appearing daughter if he could have a looksie on her iPod. Let's see how sensitive she really is. Let's make sure there's no R. "the Tinkler" Kelly, Snoop Dogg, 50 Cent, or any other artist who's made degrading remarks about hos on there. Or perhaps Reverend Slandering Colostomy Bag could have brought the daughter of Steven Pagones in and apologized to her for publicly accusing her father of dropping a deuce on the titties of a raped teenager. And then he should have kicked Whoopi Goldberg in the ass for running her fucking yap when her own production company was called One Ho Productions.

I also thought MSNBC and CBS were completely ridiculous to fire him. Fuck the advertisers. Product boycotts for this kind of shit NEVER work. It's not Selma in the 1960s, you sissies (if it were, the cause would be legitimate, and Sharpton wouldn't be involved). People aren't going to stop using toilet paper to wipe their asses, or start washing their dishes with saliva, or refuse to drink Coke because Imus made fun of a bunch of below average looking broads. Predictably, Reverend White Guy Hairdo wasn't the only shithead to go after him, there were quite a few leeches who drank the (grape) Kool-Aid right along with him.

You can't help but love the fact that Sharpton actually considered himself as a possible presidential candidate in 2003. I probably would have voted for him, provided his first act as president was to take a slow ride through Dealey Plaza.

The attention whore meets the picture whore.

I Hate Your Guts

A FEW SOLUTIONS THE GOOD REVEREND MAY WISH TO EMPLOY IN THE SPIRIT OF RECONCILIATION:

- The next time you feel the need to protest, do so dressed as an elk in Ted Nugent's backyard.
- As you read aloud grand jury testimony from the Abner Louima case, begin masturbating furiously behind the podium.
- Force Tawana Brawley to watch "2 Girls 1 Cup" while sitting on a garbage bag and eating chocolate mousse.
- Publicly acknowledge that white vaginas smell better than black ones.
- Always walk like Redd Foxx when he was feigning a heart attack in *Sanford and Son*.
- Let Imus shit in your mouth.
- Stage an impromptu pray-in and drop to your knees in the path of an oncoming A train. (Or, more appropriately, an N train.)
- Admit that you can't understand a fucking word that Jesse Jackson says.
- Demand five dollars from Bernie Goetz.

Starbucks Employees— Thanks a Latte

YOU'LL NOTICE that I didn't say Starbucks, but Starbucks employees. I am not one of those shitheads who thinks it's rebellious to attack a coffee chain. I love these ultra-left retarded protesters who target them: "Too many Starbucks popping up, maahhhhhnnn. They're bad because they're a big corporation, maahhhhhnnn. They all look the same; what about the mom-and-pop coffee places, maahhhhhnnn?" Fuck you, fuck your hatred of "the Machine," and fuck mom-and-pop coffee places.

Mom-and-pop coffee places eat ass. I tried supporting them but got sick of muddy, shitty eight-hour-old coffee. If mom and pop are going to let the coffee get stale, then mom and pop can suck my dick. There's nothing worse than drinking that horrid, bitter sludge at the bottom of the pot, which results in coffee grounds leaking down your throat. It's very similar to drinking hot water after it's been strained through used diapers. You can usually tell just by looking at it, although I can't describe exactly how. The color is just . . . off. It's too dark and appears sickly (picture normal drinking water that's been diagnosed with pancreatic cancer).

Sometimes asking how old the coffee is helps. If they immediately reply that it's freshly made, chances are it is. If you ask when it was made and they pick up a calendar, splash the scalding remainder of it in their face and skip out of the store knowing you've done the right thing.

I've also had enough of 7-Eleven and Wawa coffee and their shitty self-serve stations with dull, mucky coffee and serving areas that look like the scene of a homicide. Half the time I expect Bill Curtis to come out and describe how a hitchhiker was slaughtered behind the decaf.

And nothing irritates me more than those putrid "flavored creamer" displays. Hazelnut, Irish cream, praline, raspberry cream: all of them are disgusting and taste like they were designed specifically to overcompensate for rotten coffee. And they're on the counter in those cheap boxes—how do they not get sour? They're cream products for fuck's sake and they're being left unrefrigerated on a counter. Are they mixed with formaldehyde to prevent spoiling? A lot of times they are indeed spoiled. You ever pour in the creamer and then see white chunks floating all over in the cup five seconds later? That means spoiled. Either that, or somebody just blew a snot rocket into your beverage.

I can't tell you how many times I've driven away from one of these shithouses, taken the lid off my cup and seen icebergs bobbing in my coffee. Truly repulsive. Personally, I prefer skim milk, but I can understand people's affinity for half-and-half. (I cannot drink it because it's a thick, mucousy liquid that has me constantly clearing my throat more than the defendant in a child abduction case.) Half-and-half's tastiness aside, if it's been getting warm sitting in a cardboard box, it probably has the freshness and nutritional value of monkey cum. And nothing says appetizing fresh-roasted coffee like a giant thermos with a push button on top of it, like the septic tank of a rest area toilet.

And I'm not even going to comment on gas station coffee (or, as I say around my black friends, I am not *even* gonna go there). But I have no hard feelings, because gas stations are not supposed to have fresh, delicious beverages. Gas stations are for getting fuel and using bathrooms that have truck driver shit smeared on the mirrors. If you go to an Exxon for coffee, and only partially coagulated liquid comes out of the pot, consider yourself ahead of the game. For freshness, you're better off asking someone to drink a cup of Wawa Colombian blend and piss it into your mouth.

For some people this is not an issue. Some people can drink any coffee from anywhere, regardless of its freshness or temperature. I've known guys who could find a cold cup of coffee loaded with cigarette butts and savor it like they were sipping an espresso at the White House Correspondents' Dinner. I am admittedly a prima donna.

Which brings me to my favorite coffee: Starbucks. And when I say Starbucks, I don't mean Seattle's Best (even though it's a subsidiary of Starbucks) or that shitty Caribou Coffee. Nor will I acknowledge the Coffee Beanery, and you Canadians can take your Tim Hortons and shove them up your collective ass. For many years, I was a Dunkin' Donuts fan, but then the chain got bought out by a bunch of you-know-whats who decided to leave their Dell customer-service jobs, and now the coffee tastes stale and dingy. And I haven't bought a cup from McDonald's since that old lady spilled some on her crotch, burned her meat flaps, and sued for $2 million.

There is a reason that I am so brand loyal, and it isn't because of Starbucks' dopey logo, believe me. I cannot, for the life of me, figure out what message they are trying to convey with that horrible symbol. It's a green circle with a longhaired mermaid-looking broad in it. And she's wearing that stupid multipointed hat. I'd love to meet her and scream, "Nice hat, cunt!" as I spin kick it off her fucking head.

And I can't figure out if those are supposed to be her arms next to her crowding the inside of the circle. They look like the witch's legs sticking out from under the house in *The Wizard of Oz* with two weird flippers on the end of them. Whenever I see her, I think of those icky lobster-handed people I saw on the Discovery Channel. Apparently this lobster-hand thing is hereditary. Which begs the question: If you had unpleasant lobstery hands, wouldn't you have the common courtesy to stop fucking? Or at the very least, pull out and cum on your wife's back (or dorsal fin)? How do these claw-fingered zilches live with themselves knowing that everyone who meets them wants to soak their hands in warm butter and eat them? If nothing else, the Starbucks mermaid must give a monumentally bad hand job. I can't imagine anything worse than being jerked off by someone without fingers (except relying on them to type a memo or put in your contact lenses).

The logo they use now is the second incarnation of a similar image. The original version (which was brought back recently for promotional purposes) showed a fuller view of the mermaid. She's sitting in the middle of that circle, holding each of her two "tails" up in the air at shoulder height. Whether you want to call them tails or legs, they're wide open. Apparently nothing says "fresh coffee" like open, exposed mermaid pussy.

My reason for such brand loyalty is, as I've said, a separate issue. I like their coffee products. A lot. One of my favorite beverages is the iced latte, and for some reason only Starbucks gets it right. I find the other companies to have enragingly watery iced lattes, and on more than one occasion I've had to fight the urge to spill my drink on the floor and set the entrance on fire. Nothing gets my goat (pardon my French) like a watery iced latte. I also fancy a Frappuccino every now and again, although I tend to avoid them because they have the same fat content as a chocolate-covered ham.

The distinction between hating the product and the employees is an important one. Normally I'll order a medium coffee with skim milk, which at my local Starbucks in New York comes to about $2.02. I never have exact change, as I was raised to believe that pennies are for faggots.

So I will produce three crisp singles, and hand them over with a flourish. I then stick my other hand out stiffly to receive my change—because I know change is coming. One of the main reasons I hate the employees is because those penny-pinching shitdicks will actually hand me back ninety-eight cents instead of just letting me beat the system for two pennies. As the pile of change drops into my hand, in one beautifully fluid motion, I angle my hand down over the cup with TIPS written on it, and generously allow ninety-eight cents *that is rightfully mine* to slip effortlessly into it. And they say the same thing every time, "Can I help the next guest please?" Can you help the next guest? First of all, stop calling us guests. We are not guests, you smug imbeciles; we are slobs who are overpaying for an admittedly tasty beverage. A guest is someone you invite over, who enjoys a cup of coffee they don't have to refinance their home for.

Second, and more important, before you help the next "guest," how about you say "thank you" to the guest who just gave you a 49 percent tip? How about one goddamn moment of common courtesy to acknowledge that someone else who works for a living just handed over some extra money when you did *nothing* extra to earn it? This has obviously not been a one-time occurrence; it happens almost every time I drop any change or even bills into that bottomless tip cup. The entitled snots behind the counter receive their gift without an ounce of gratitude and quickly move on to the next mindless idiot.

I am not deluded into thinking I'm a philanthropist leaving a life-changing endowment. I'm just one jerk-off in a long line of jerk-offs trying to quickly grab a beverage that will help me shit more efficiently. I am not expecting tears of joy, confetti from the ceiling, or a hand job in the stock room. How about just a "Thank you. May I help the next customer?" Or guest, fuck it. I'll accept guest if you just throw a thank-you in there somewhere.

Perhaps, since the counter employees are far too progressive to be concerned with the banality of courtesy, how about you just hire one older gentleman to stand at the door and thank everybody on the way out? This way, the people behind the register can be the rude, self-centered Emo hipsters they're comfortable being, and I can exit without a burning resentment, mumbling to myself how it's the last time I'm leaving those assholes anything. It's a small thing, but a generation (yes, I am playing the generation card) of brats who are used to being handed things from Mommy and Daddy is making me sick to my soft, pasty stomach. And my issue isn't that they're being handed things either. I was certainly handed things by Mommy and Daddy, all the time. And when my hands were too full, I'd reach out and grab for more with my feet. To be honest, I was a spoiled little cunt. However, I always said *please* and I always said *thank you*. Always.

As a way of combating these little pricks, I've found that buying the Starbucks gift cards is the way to go. I usually put fifty bucks on them, and smile knowing not one dime of that is going to be wasted as an unappreciated tip (unless they get a cut of every gift card sold, in which case I'll protest by slitting my own throat like a lamb and bleeding out over the Ethos water display). My anger has completely vanished now that I can just hand over a card and get it back, not expecting a thank-you and, of course, not receiving one.

Another major point of contention with these people is the fact that they call themselves Baristas. What the fuck is a Barista? And more important, why am I capitalizing it? I looked it up in the dictionary and it doesn't exist. The only pseudodefinition I found was on Wikipedia, where it says "barista" refers to one who has acquired some level of expertise in the preparation of espresso-based coffee drinks. Huh? This is a joke, right? Doesn't this imply that every twat-face with a Nespresso machine is a potential barista? And for the record, the next time I order a medium and the passive-aggressive bag of shit behind the counter repeats it back as "Okay, one grande coffee" (subtly correcting me), I'm going to smile politely, mosey out to my car, and drive it through the front window like the Terminator.

In conclusion, I'd also like to petition the corporate offices to redesign the current model of lids in circulation. For some reason, every time I take a sip, cold coffee drips from underneath the lip of the lid onto the back of my hand. I'll be goddamned if I know why, but after I take a sip, a small amount of coffee stays up under the lid and sneaks out over the ridge of the cup to the outside lip of the lid. As the cup leaves my lips and heads back down, without fail that cocksucking, motherfucking drop of coffee will leak out onto my hand. And every time it happens, I become filled with a homicidal rage. I am not exaggerating. On numerous occasions I've driven my car while holding a cup of Starbucks away from my body screaming "Fuck you!" at it. One time, I actually spit full force onto the cup (as well as on my thumb and the dashboard) while screaming "You fucking piece . . . of . . . shit!" so loudly I blew out my voice. Ironically, the cup answered back by leaking another fresh drop of cold coffee onto my knuckle. (I jotted that one down in the loss column.) I'm surprised the cup didn't say TIPS on it.

CUSTOMER RELATIONS IMPROVEMENT TIPS:

- Train your employees to say "thank you" by attaching electrodes to their genitals.
- Make it mandatory that half of their tips are donated to Islamic Jihad or Hamas.
- Instead of "guest," the customer is to be referred to as "Massah."
- No longer permit monetary tips; if customers are satisfied

that they've received above-average service, they can express their satisfaction by diarrhetically evacuating into the TIPS cup.

- To prevent leakage and drips, stop making the lids out of the same material used for the levees in New Orleans.
- Baristas are henceforth to be referred to as "liquid colon-cleanser preparers."
- Engage me in funny banter. For instance, when I walk up to the counter, smile and ask, "Hey friend, what can I do you for?"
- Begin charging customers $300 for wireless Internet access.
- Find a way to make your "reduced fat" blueberry crumb cake less than four hundred calories so I can stop purging in the bathroom after I eat one.
- Hire a slew of those sub-human, lobster-handed weirdos, and make them stand at the front entrance with rubber bands tightly wrapped around their fingers.

People I Wanted to Kill on Sight: Part One

- The woman going through airport security in front of me this morning. She passes through the metal detector, then stops at the end of the X-ray machine to collect her carry-on bags. Instead of coming out and rolling down the belt, the rest of our bags begin piling up inside the machine while this self-centered whore puts her shoes on, and then puts her laptop back in its bag. Meanwhile, the remaining twenty feet of conveyor belt remains as unused and barren as I hope her womb is.

- The three Indian people on the plane directly behind me right now, who smell, to phrase it gently, like spicy logs of shit.

- The flight attendant who is currently scolding the Indians behind me for changing seats. She looks like Kraus from *Benson*. Although I hate the Indian family, it does not negate the fact that this flight attendant is a cunt on wheels and a control freak.

- Bachelorette parties who sit up front in comedy clubs wearing funny hats and drinking out of cups through penis straws. They're always loud and become incensed when you ask them to quiet down, and the one who answers back the loudest invariably has fat arms. Fast-forward five minutes and I'm screaming "Shut up, cunts!" with such ferocity it gives me throat polyps.

The Hillbilly Book Police

AS MIND-BOGGLING as it seems, *Happy Endings* was actually pulled from the shelves of a public library. The fact that it happened in Mississippi, however, is far less mind-boggling (unless you're boggled that Mississippi has libraries). That's right, folks, the same state that gave us great American comedies like *Mississippi Burning* had an issue with my book. Way to dispel those myths about the South, you fucking hayseeds.

I was alerted to this fact mid-September of 2007 via an email with a link to a local newspaper article. Apparently the Jackson-George Regional Library System Director, Michael Hamlett, decided to remove my book from the shelves after an obscenity complaint from ONE patron. ONE person, and this spineless prick decides to yank it. This particular library system consists of eight branches and two counties, totaling *forty-five thousand people.*

After removing the book, Hamlett reviewed it, and then stored it in his asshole for safety. Then this milquetoast fairy had meetings with the library staff and members of the board, and asked these people to review the book and give recommendations. What a pansy. I read that he could have made the decision to return it to the shelves himself after his "review." I hate this noncommittal scumbag. All he had to do was look through it to realize there's nothing pornographic about it. If this vacuous jellyfish can't peruse a hardcover book and differentiate between comedic essays and pornography, then he's far too stupid to be in any position of authority in a library system. Ironically, the last book removed from the shelves of this backward shithole was *America* by Jon Stewart. After numerous complaints, the library buckled and put that offensive, morally damaging Comedy Central filth back on the shelves.

When asked about *Happy Endings*, library system spokesman Rex Bridges really irritated me when he commented, "I don't know where it was, but all the copies are under review and have been taken out of circulation. I don't think it's a popular title. When we buy, we usually buy popular titles. This may have been on a reading list and purchased." Not a popular title, huh? It was number four on the *New York Times* bestseller list, you borderline retarded shitkicker. Sorry that isn't popular enough for you. Do the highbrows in your library system only purchase the top three on the list? Or are you just running that toothy cum-holder in the middle of your face without knowing what the hell you're talking about? Be a good little boy and do your goddamn homework before you talk to the press, asshole.

Rex further annoyed me when he said he could not state the basis for the complaint or give even a general idea of the patron's objection. Of course he couldn't. Do they tell this idiot anything, or does he just wing it whenever there's a microphone in his face? The options were to send the book to the board or return it to the shelves. Mr. Well Informed then stated that the book would only be considered banned and removed from the system if the board voted that way. And, in reference to the process of reviewing complaints, Bridges answered, "We don't have too many examples of doing this. It doesn't happen very often." Wow, that's a relief. In America, in 2007, they don't yank too many books off the shelves for objectionable material. Whew. Hopefully they'll come around and start accepting other nutty ideas, like interracial relationships and rock music. And not only could he not be specific about the complaint, he wouldn't name the cocksucker who complained. Therein lies a major problem in our country: a lack of accountability. People always seem to feel more comfortable complaining like sniveling pussies in the comfort of anonymity.

Conclusion

At their big September 25 meeting, the board, being the mensches they are, decided not to ban *Happy Endings*. But they also refused to return it to the shelves. They made the book available, but only on request. This is, of course, a form of censoring it. The only reason they didn't ban it outright was because of the amount of shit they'd have caught for removing it from circulation.

Whether you liked *Happy Endings* or not, it was an honest collection of writings about my life, all meant to be funny. Once again, some stiff, self-will-imposing cowards have attacked something done in humor in an attempt to appear to be "getting something done." Had these been autobiographical tales about drug abuse, violence, or prison, these felched assholes would have considered the confessions courageous. The disdain I feel for them is almost indescribable.

Herr Direktor Hamlett commented that since my book is only in less than three hundred libraries, "that should tell you something." Yes, piss gargler, it does. It tells you that jerk-offs like you work in library systems all over the country. It tells you that a book that remained on the *New York Times* bestseller list for a total of five weeks doesn't merit being on their shelves due to objectionable content. And it also tells you that the stereotype about librarians being uptight, humorless old biddies is true. I just didn't realize that it also applied to male librarians. You're a man doing a woman's job; you should be forced to show up to work wearing hose and a girdle every day, you vagina-wielding hen.

Incidentally, of the four members, one voted to ban it. The piece of shit in question is a guy named David Ogborn. He thinks *Happy Endings* should have been banned because, "I'm a director of a library, not an adult book club. That kind of garbage there, I don't think it belongs in the library. You can call it censorship or anything you want to but there's a difference in right and wrong and that's wrong."

A couple of things here. First of all, there's no such thing as an "adult book club," you stupid, insular bumpkin. When people want adult material, we go online and masturbate into a sock, or mosey into an adult bookstore to get blown through a hole in the wall.

Point number two: I take umbrage with my literary masterpiece being called "garbage." *Nonsense*, *malarkey*, *balderdash*, and *tomfoolery* are all acceptable. *Garbage* is just plain mean, and I'd be less than honest if I said it didn't hurt my feelings.

Third point: we can call it censorship, and will call it that, because that's what it is, you fat, bald rube. What you don't seem to understand is that your taste in entertainment should not outweigh someone else's right to enjoy it. This is a depressing argument to be having in such modern times, when we can not only send a man to the moon, but when he returns, we can film a horse fucking him to death.

Fourth, and most important, is that you're correct—there is a difference between right and wrong. RIGHT: understanding that you're an old man and what you find acceptable is irrelevant. You're from an overrated generation who not only kept blacks from voting, but thought *My Favorite Martian* was funny. WRONG: voting to ban a book because it describes sexual activities you'd be well advised to try with your spouse.

While it seems incidents like this are certainly not as common as they used to be, they still happen far more frequently than they should. The only books that should encounter issues like these are self-help manuals on the subject of titanium anal beads that wind up in the children's section.

I Hate Your Guts

A FEW OTHER BANNED AND
CHALLENGED BOOKS IN 2007:

- *Of Mice and Men.* Challenged for classroom use in New-
  ton, Iowa; Humble Independent School District, Texas;
  Appomattox County, Virginia; and Olathe, Kansas. Banned
  in Appling County, Georgia. How could anyone ban this
  book? It teaches valuable lessons, like tolerance for big re-
  tards and how to best dispose of an old dog.

- *The Adventures of Huckleberry Finn.* Challenged in schools
  in Minneapolis, Minnesota; Dallas, Texas; and Manchester,
  Connecticut, by a white woman named Nigger Jim.

- *It's Perfectly Normal: Changing Bodies, Growing Up, Sex,
  and Sexual Health.* Checked out and not returned as a
  means of challenge in Lewiston, Maine, public libraries.
  More than likely, this was removed by some religious zealot
  who enjoys the feeling of a young boy's hiney wrapped
  around his turgid erection. (Phrasing it like that actually
  makes it sound pretty jim-dandy to the rest of us, too.)
  Either that, or it was removed because it violated the age-
  old rule of a book having less than two hundred words in
  the title.

- *Happy Endings: The Tales of a Meaty-Breasted Zilch.* Considered by many to be the best written book on the 2007
  banned and challenged list. Challenged in public libraries
  in Mississippi by an anonymous incest survivor with a pen-
  chant for holding animal shit in his mouth.

- *Medical Ethics: Moral and Legal Conflicts in Health Care (Issues for the 90s).* Challenged in Palm Beach, Florida, by a mother who searched the card catalog for terms she found objectionable. She challenged this book *in addition to seventy-nine other titles.* I don't know who this woman is, but I hope her cancer of the uterus pain is temporarily being forgotten due to the agony of the four large, melanin-covered dicks currently being forced into her anus.

- *Wizardology: The Book of the Secrets of Merlin (Ologies).* Challenged in West Haven, Connecticut, for inclusion in an elementary school library. The man who challenged this book suddenly went blind after fucking a toad.

A FEW THINGS OVER-FIFTY LIBRARY EMPLOYEES SHOULD UNDERSTAND ABOUT HUMOR:

1. You know virtually nothing about it. NO ONE thinks you're funny unless you're burning yourself with soup or shattering a hip on an icy driveway.

2. Shows you enjoyed while growing up didn't have more integrity because people refrained from using "salty language." They didn't use it simply because they weren't allowed to. But I am, so fuck yourself in the ass with a big stick.

3. Dewey Decimal System references are only funny in the context of a rape joke.

4. Gracie Allen saying, "Goodnight, Gracie," isn't funny now, nor was it ever.

5. If you've ever laughed at a story someone told about accidentally putting a reference book in the fiction section, place this book on the counter, walk out to the parking lot, get in your car, and drive it into a cement wall.

6. The funniest thing that happens in a library is when a man in silk running shorts is arrested for masturbating while viewing pornography on one of your computers.

Steve Martin—
a Real Piece of Merde

STEVE MARTIN has earned a spot in this book, and not for that stupid half-Asian squint he does on every movie poster. I'm not saying that smug face he makes isn't enough to land him a chapter, but that's not what ultimately did it. No, Steve's crime against humanity was accepting the starring role in *The Pink Panther*. And not only did he accept the role, he annihilated it. He couldn't have made me laugh less if he were playing Inspector Clouseau in *Schindler's List*. It was almost a thing of technical beauty the way he completely removed every ounce of charisma, charm, and humor from a character that Peter Sellers did so brilliantly. Steve Martin's version was ninety-three minutes of contrived, unfunny garbage. Even the accent wasn't funny; it was the type of douchey French accent your friend uses at a party to make a drunk girl laugh before she pukes on his dick.

I got so angry watching this hunk of shit because Steve Martin is in a position to pick and choose the roles he wants. He can wait for an original script instead of putting on the clothes of a dead comedic prodigy and shallowly parading around doing shitty, humorless sight gags. Any comedian worth his weight in stomach bile would have refused this role out of respect for Sellers's legend, out of respect for the fact that the role of Clouseau should forever be his and his alone. But no, not this pompous ass. He couldn't throw on the funny hat and pencil-thin asshole mustache fast enough. And what's even worse is knowing that a horrendous sequel is undoubtedly right around the corner, like a recurring dose of rectal cancer. If the sequel bombs at the box office perhaps he can poison Jim Carrey and redo *Ace Ventura* or *The Cable Guy*. I'm surprised he didn't exhume Sellers's body and rifle through his pockets while he was at it.

And that excuse of "it's a great role, I wanted to bring something new to it" is also unabashed bullshit. How would you feel if another comic put on a white suit and ran around like a retard with an arrow through his head? Would you think, *Gee, what a flattering and amusing tribute to a role I created?* No, of course you wouldn't. You'd think, *Hey, that fucking asshole is stealing my shit.* And you'd be right.

What did I do when I met Steve Martin, you ask? Did I shit talk him to his face? You bet I didn't. I took a nice crystal-clear picture and then shamefacedly wormed my way back up to my hotel room.

This is not a role that needs to be remade due to improvements in special effects, you idiot. You want to redo a film? Put on a monkey mask, tell everyone you're Mighty Joe Young, and throw handfuls of your own feces at every *Pink Panther* movie poster in town.

In the spirit of fairness, Steve is not solely responsible for this comedic abomination—he had plenty of assistance. So, in addition to him, I've added a few more people who should also be buried up to the neck in a septic tank for their participation:

- Steve Martin. Steve gets a second nod for not only starring in, but also cowriting the hideous screenplay. Going into it, I assumed the premise would be some cunty scavenger hunt involving an oversize diamond; I wasn't expecting *Dr. Zhivago*. What I didn't expect was that every joke, without exception, would be based on curtains being torn down, a man falling off a bicycle, or something bouncing up into someone's penis. Don't get me wrong—I enjoy nothing more than watching something bounce up into someone's penis (particularly if the bouncing object is covered with carpenter nails or on fire). But this was just pathetic, more in the vein of the Special Olympics (minus the Moe Howard haircuts and embarrassed relatives). They even wrote in a scene where Inspector Clouseau gets his hand caught in two vases, which was predictably terrible. When Peter Sellers would get his hand caught in things, it was hilarious. When Steve Martin gets his hand caught in something, you find yourself wishing it was the clenched asshole of a diving blue whale.

- Kevin Kline earns a spot on the shit list thanks to his dull, uninspired portrayal of Chief Inspector Dreyfus. His performance had the humor value of a Civil War reenactment. Instead of being a twitchy borderline sociopath like Herbert Lom in the original films, he was just boring Kevin Kline, but with a French accent. He's obviously a seasoned actor; he proved that by delivering his lines instead of running through the table reads with an axe.

- Beyoncé Knowles, for being the "black audience draw" cast member in this dud. Since Steve Martin has less of a fan base among black moviegoers than Jim Crow, the only way to get black people in theaters to see him portray a bungling Frenchman is to add a high-profile black celebrity. Beyoncé not only covers the black audience draw but the sex appeal angle as well. I don't need sex appeal in a comedy. Fat women are naturally funnier, because you can always have the other characters angrily moo at her whenever she enters a room. I either want to laugh or jerk off, never both. And in the case of this movie, neither. I don't hate Beyoncé, although anyone who saw this film just because of her certainly should.

- Peter Sellers, for dying. Thanks for nothing, stupid. You create one of the funniest characters of all time and then decide to drop dead of a massive coronary at fifty-five? What the fuck was your heart made of, paraffin? Some time on the treadmill, a few less sticks of butter, and we could have avoided this whole goddamn mess.

In the end, this cinematic equivalent of rhinoceros shit made more than $80 million at the box office. Shows you how much I know. The worse I think a comedy is, the more Americans rush to see it. And this isn't about claiming that Steve Martin sucks, he's done some tremendously funny films, in addition to being one of the funniest performers ever to appear on *SNL*. He was also my favorite Oscars host, and on top of all that, a good writer. So I'm not saying his body of work as a whole is shit. It isn't. Just everything he's done since 1987.

IF STEVE WANTS TO MAKE THINGS RIGHT AGAIN, PERHAPS HE SHOULD "INSPECT" THESE SUGGESTIONS:

- Dress up like Inspector Clouseau and get arrested in a *Dateline NBC* sting.
- Write a remake of *Roots* where Chicken George dresses and talks like Inspector Clouseau without explanation.
- Strap explosives to your chest and spice up your next big premiere with a suicide bombing.
- If Beyoncé is in the sequel, have her do a nude scene where she rapes Inspector Clouseau with a strap-on.
- Have the next *Pink Panther* plot revolve around Clouseau good-naturedly bumbling the Madeleine McCann case.
- Put me in one of your movies.

The Pregnant Man. Or Woman. Or Whatever the Fuck That Thing Is

I'M TIRED of this attention whore. Thomas Beatie is not a man. Thomas Beatie is a woman without tits. Having or not having tits doesn't dictate gender, or I'd be a girl and Nancy Reagan would be a boy. The tabloid shitty American media is desperately trying to make this nonsense more interesting than it is. They continue to perpetuate this nonstory because they just love writing "pregnant man." Reporters are just tickled pink at the juxtaposition of those words. In a recent *New York Post* article, the words "dad," "him," "he," and "his" are used a total of fifteen times.

Born Tracy Langolino, she began her transformation into masculinity by having her breasts flattened/removed and taking hormones. She then began the difficult part of the process by blowing out snot rockets and learning to read maps correctly. At first glance, Tracy appears to be a man (if that first glance is taken at midnight from across the street). She has a whispy beard, hairy pits, and sports a short masculine hairdo. She looks like George Michael. However, a couple of things she neglected to do were have her ovaries removed or a cock installed. Way to commit there, honey: "I want to be a man, but I want my ovaries." Oh, well then you're not a man, toots. Call me old-school, but where I come from, if you have a pussy, you're a dame. You want to be a man? Have your womb spackled shut, tinkle out of your clit, and lose your life's savings in a divorce. You can't have it both ways. Make up your goddamn mind already—you're completely indecisive. Typical woman.

Now we're being subjected to this moronic Demi Moore-ish picture of Thomas caressing her pregnant belly. The press has been classifying her relationship with her partner, Nancy, as "unorthodox," but meanwhile, they're just a couple of lesbians. What in Sam Hill is so unorthodox about that? They tried having kids in 2006, but she miscarried with triplets. The obvious disadvantage to triplets in the womb is that they can talk things over and put two and two together: "Hey, do you smell cigar smoke?" "Yes, and I also hear dirty jokes being followed by laughter." "Shit, I think we're inside a guy. Let's get the fuck out of here. . . ." I don't feel it was a miscarriage as much as it was a prison break.

To get around the whole "men can't have babies, you fucking moron" argument, she responds, "Wanting to have a child is neither a male or female desire, but a human desire." Great. Flying isn't a bird's desire, but a living creature's desire. Toss yourself off the Chrysler Building and see how that works out for you. Desire to carry a child, plus cock and balls, equals tough shit.

That kid should have a terrific time in school: "My dad was a woman, then became a man, until she decided to get pregnant with me." This isn't beautiful or a sign of true love, this is a perfect example of a wavering, wishy-washy broad who needs people in her life who love her enough to tell her what a total ass she's making out of herself. She's babbling about the "right to have a biological child." I don't think anyone's debating her legal right. But if we're going to be subjected to this pathetic display of exhibitionism, then we have the right to point, laugh, and say, "Ha, ha, you're no man—you're just an ugly chick with a beard." If childbirth is that important to you as a couple, then *let the voted-on woman in the relationship have it*. In this case, her partner, Nancy, is unable to conceive because after pumping out two kids during her first marriage, she had her uterus removed. (The downside is, she cannot have a child in this second marriage. The good news is she and Thomas have a great place to store their winter coats.) I still don't see the big deal. I'm a big supporter of gay adoption, so instead of subjecting the rest of us to your obsession with chronic uniqueness, why don't you and your gal pal head over to Sudan and grab yourselves a trophy like every other attention-seeking media whore?

Americans have developed this enraging infatuation with the concepts of blind tolerance and how labels of any kind, regardless of accuracy, are bad. Beatie told Oprah in an exclusive interview (since she's trying to keep a low profile), "I see pregnancy as a process and it doesn't define who I am." In the sense of being a Democrat or Republican, good point. But it most certainly does define your gender, stupid ass. And if this isn't about getting attention for yourself, then stop telling everyone you're a pregnant man. Just shut up about the whole thing and no one will even look at you twice; they'll just assume you're a falsetto-voiced guy with a fat gut.

The pregnancy occured with sperm from an unknowing donor. Some creep on the subway wacked his bag onto the back of her dress, and a light switched on in her head. I'm kidding, of course! Nancy inseminated her using a syringelike device, and I imagine the procedure resembled dripping Bausch & Lomb rewetting drops into Sandy Duncan's eye socket. They bought the device from a veterinarian, and it's typically used to feed birds. Ewww. I wonder if her vag lips quivered and gripped the end of the syringe like a newly hatched ostrich.

They saw *nine* obstetricians before they found one willing to help.

What the hell does that tell you? Almost every twat doctor in Oregon told them to hit the bricks. Thomas claimed that "doctors have discriminated against us, turning us away due to their religious beliefs." I don't know if you can blame this one on religion, honey. You walk into a doctor's office with a beard, introduce yourself as Thomas, then ask if they can check your snatch because you want to have a baby. You don't exactly have to be an Islamist extremist to find that odd.

She said she couldn't wait to see her baby's face. Me neither. I'd have given my right arm to get a gander at that kid's expression when she popped out, took a peek over the clit, and saw Jack Black staring down at her. And good luck with breastfeeding there, selfish. Her poor daughter will clamp down on one of those nipples and have the same look on her face that I get when I realize the SunnyD container is empty.

A FEW CREEPY THINGS THAT WILL BE OVERHEARD IN THE BEATIE HOUSEHOLD:

- "Hey, Pop, close the hole in your boxers, your pussy's showing."
- "I told you to clean your room, young lady! Just wait until your father finishes changing his tampon."
- "I had lizard cum sprayed onto my ovaries; I'm going to be the world's first man who gives birth to a reptile baby. Get Oprah on the phone."
- "I got grounded, my parents are having their periods."

Oscar the Douche

IT'S TOO bad that Oscar is just a statue and not an actual guy who you can punch in the face. Or, at the very least, fire for incompetence. Over the years there have been so many horrible decisions made, it's miraculous some actor hasn't stood up in the middle of the ceremony with an AR-15 to set the record straight.

A lot of people don't give a shit about the Oscars, and put zero emotional investment into who wins. And it's not just certain members of the public; there are actors who feel that way as well. I'm talking about good actors, of course. No one gives a shit what Keanu Reeves thinks about the Oscars, simply because he has the same shot at winning one as I do.

Marlon Brando is a great example of someone who has not only embraced the Academy, but also spit back in its face. He was victim to a terrible decision in 1951, after being nominated for *A Streetcar Named Desire* and losing to Humphrey Bogart in *The African Queen*. Yuck. Humphrey Bogart was okay, but overrated; he was one of those old-school straight-delivery actors with "Why dontcha go on and scram, see," that type of shit. A one-level cardboard cutout when compared to a young Brando. Or maybe it was just a sign of the times: it's much easier to hand out an Oscar to a guy who played a riverboat captain helping a missionary lady than to a drunken alpha male who rapes his wife's cunty sister in an apartment without air-conditioning.

Brando was also nominated and lost the following year to Gary Cooper. Another fine thespian that Brando could method-act circles around. In 1953, he was nominated and lost again, this time to William Holden (see prior two acting analyses). By this point, he must have been feeling like Susan Lucci. Oh, wait . . . we're talking early 1950s, Susan Lucci is an inaccurate reference. Let me rephrase that: by this point, he must have been feeling like every black actor. Much better.

The following year he finally wins for *On the Waterfront*. Fast-forward eighteen years and one more lost nomination later, and he wins for *The Godfather*. What a difference a couple of decades makes. Instead of showing up, he sends some chick dressed like an American Indian to accept it for him. The crowd began booing, so she started slapping her palm against her mouth and "woo-woo-wooing" in a circle like an asshole until it rained all over everyone. The best part is that she wasn't even an Indian, but some dopey actress.

It's amazing how they all booed, yet politicizing the Oscars became immensely popular in years to follow. (George C. Scott actually refused it for *Patton* two years before. But as far as I know, he gave a dignified answer about "every actor not having played the same role" instead of sending some left-wing weirdo dressed for a game of cowboys and Indians.) I've obviously rambled on about Marlon the Fatso enough, so to further prove my point, I'm listing many more of the shitty decisions made by the Academy. . . .

1974

Arguably the worst decision ever made by the Academy: Best Actor goes *not* to Al Pacino for *The Godfather: Part II* but to Art Carney for *Harry and Tonto*. Were those cocksuckers out of their minds? Best Cure for Insomnia maybe. Who the fuck voted that year, Jackie Gleason, Audrey Meadows, and Joyce Randolph?

If I were the presenter, I'd have just said Pacino's name anyway and took my chances. *Harry and Tonto* is a quaint feel-good movie about an old man who drives cross-country with his cat. The sentimental grandmothers who gave this award to Art Carney should have just handed him a baggie of petrified cat shit instead. They screwed Pacino, and as a result, had to screw another actor years later. Apparently it's more palatable to reward a doddering, pussy cat–loving old codger than a ruthless mafia don who has his own brother shot while trying to catch a fish. Makes perfect sense! Fuck Oscar.

1979

While not as disgusting as 1974, this year they decided to rob Peter Sellers after his amazing performance in *Being There.* He played a borderline retarded gardener who winds up advising some of the most powerful men in the country. It's funny and he played it brilliantly. (And I'm eagerly awaiting Steve Martin's interpretation of this role. Will be interesting to see it played totally devoid of humor.) As the credits were rolling, the complete dolt of a director, Hal Ashby, showed a blooper reel like it was a prequel to *The Cannonball Run.* I heard Sellers was furious, and told Ashby he'd just cost him an Oscar. Certainly possible.

That year it went to Dustin Hoffman for *Kramer vs. Kramer.* Good movie, but was he better than Sellers? NO, silly geese, he wasn't. Good-hearted single dad is just an easier guy to root for, I guess. *Kramer vs. Kramer* also beat out *Apocalypse Now* for Best Picture. Go shit in your hat. I laughed heartily when shitty li'l Billy fell off the jungle gym and needed stitches. Then again, I jerked off when Colonel Kurtz dropped a decapitated head in Martin Sheen's lap. Maybe I'm the problem.

1980

This year saw not only the worst decision ever made by the Academy, but perhaps the worst decision ever made by human beings. Best Picture goes to . . . *Raging Bu* . . . huh? No? It goes to what? *Ordinary People*? Are you sure? These DUMB MOTHERFUCKERS actually gave the Oscar to *Ordinary People* over *Raging Bull*. *Raging Bull* was a masterpiece, easily the best film of the decade. *Ordinary People* was good, but Best Picture? You limp-wristed swishes. And then to prove that it was no mistake, they give Robert Redford Best Director over Scorsese. Scorsese's direction, the camera work, the sounds—it was a perfect directing job. *Citizen Kane* can lick my fucking ball bag. And so can Redford. And so can De Niro and Scorsese while we're at it. Fuck everyone.

1981

The idiots only got if half right this year. Best Actor and Actress went to Henry Fonda and Katharine Hepburn for *On Golden Pond*. All right, you got me, I'm a washwoman and I cry every time I see this goddamn movie. It's absolutely great. They deserved their Oscars. Very rarely do I consider an actor brave, but Hepburn chasing loons around a pond while her head was almost bobbling itself into Gimbal lock certainly took balls.

Then, the Academy goes and gives Best Picture to *Chariots of Fire*. Sweet Jesus, why? Who gives a shit about a bunch of jogging butt pirates? I imagine this movie won because certain Academy members couldn't keep their hands off their dicks while they were watching it.

1984

Amadeus won Best Picture over *A Soldier's Story*. It shouldn't have. Blacks get so fucked during the Oscars, and have for so long that you can't call it bad luck or paranoia. This was a film with a bunch of relatively unknown (at the time) black actors, including Denzel Washington. It was about a black sergeant who is killed on a military base, and at first glance it appears the culprits are white officers. (One of the white officers is played by Wings Hauser, who also brilliantly portrayed a pimp named Ramrod in a fine little feature called *Vice Squad*. In it, he beats MTV's Nina Blackwood to death with a coat hanger, and stabs Rerun from *What's Happening!!* in the balls with a switchblade. To call this one a laugh riot would be an understatement.)

A Soldier's Story deals with a lot of interesting racial issues, especially about how blacks see one another and the way they judge one another's behavior around whites. A great film. So why did *Amadeus* win it? Because, obviously, a bunch of irritating old crackers in white powdered wigs was infinitely more fascinating to the Academy, and Mozart's life story was, of course, safer content. You'll notice the Academy only likes to see blacks in certain roles. That's right ladies and germs—I'm turning into a bleeding-heart, knee-jerk reactionary liberal douchebag right in front of your very eyes! Quick—somebody give me a kick in the cunt to shut me up!

1985

Another year, another shit decision. *Out of Africa* wins Best Picture over *The Color Purple*. *Out of Africa* was a fucking borefest, starring Meryl Streep and Robert Redford, about some stupid white bitch who gets cheated on by her husband, catches VD from him, then learns how wonderful African culture is. Zzzzzzzz. I was on the husband's side the entire time.

The Color Purple, on the other hand, is a whimsical slapstick comedy, starring Oprah Winfrey and Whoopi Goldberg as two sisters who are also detectives. Danny Glover plays the cranky over-the-hill sergeant who just wants to retire quietly. SPOILER ALERT! The film ends with a hot air balloon chase set to the theme music from *The Benny Hill Show*. And it goes without saying: no Oscar for Oprah or Whoopi. Sorry, black people. Aced out by whitey yet again.

1986

Platoon justifiably wins Best Picture. Had they given the award to any other film, the automatic sprinkler system in the Kodak Theatre would have turned itself on and sprayed AIDS all over the audience. (Lucky for *Platoon* Robert Redford wasn't starring in or directing one of his dismal treks through a midlife crisis.) Although they gave it Best Picture, do those assholes give a Best Supporting Actor to Tom Berenger or Willem Dafoe? If they had, I wouldn't be writing this, you idiot. They gave the award to—drum roll, please—Michael Caine for *Hannah and Her Sisters*. Sergeant Barnes should have killed Michael Caine, fucked Hannah, and then raped her sisters. Die. Die. Die. Fucking die. I still don't feel better. DIE. Now I do. Kind of.

1989

Well, the Academy took two years off and then insisted on being twats again. Best Picture absolutely should have been *Born on the Fourth of July*, not that sapfest *Driving Miss Daisy*. Fuck Morgan the chauffeur and fuck that cadaverous ofay he was lugging around. Tell Miss Daisy to pick up her pussy off the floor and go hail a cab. I was glad she died at the end. In addition, Tom Cruise should have gotten Best Actor instead of Daniel Day-Lewis playing some left-footed asshole. Denzel won Best Supporting Actor for *Glory*, which he was amazing in. (He has a better on-cue tear roll then Demi Moore.) I felt *Glory* also deserved Best Picture over *Skull Fucking Miss Daisy*. And incidentally, I'm tired of Morgan Freeman narrating every motherfucking movie he's in the exact same way. How about trying some inflection, asshole? And there's no need to rewind the tape, you heard it right. I, Jim Norton, as a direct result of my performances in *Lucky Louie*, am confidently shitting on Morgan Freeman's acting. Put that in your pipe and smoke it.

1992

This is the year I was referring to when I said that by giving Art Carney Best Actor in 1974, they were screwing Pacino, and thereby screwed another actor down the line when they had to finally make it up to Pacino. Al was finally given a Best Actor Oscar for his performance in *Scent of a Woman*. Yikes. Not a bad film, but he ran around it with a cane hoo-wahh-ing it up so much he sounded like Billy Bob in *Sling Blade*. It was a nice job, but to give it to him over Denzel Washington in *Malcolm X* is just embarrassing. He was amazing as Malcolm X; he humanized a guy that most white people, me included, had always heard was a heartless, radical prick. I cried at the end of that movie (nothing to do with the film, two gentlemen of color pinched my girlfriend's shitter and then assaulted me for my jujubes).

This was also a slap at Spike Lee, who didn't even get nominated for Best Director, nor did *X* get nominated for Best Picture. An absolute disgrace. The Academy just hates Spike; he's never been given a Best Director nomination for a film. The only nomination he got was for the *Do the Right Thing* screenplay, which lost to *Dead Poets Society*. Are you really surprised? Once again, a bunch of upper crust, blue-eyed devils rewarding themselves and their own suburban angst. Not your typical Robin Williams comedy (although it was funny when Neil put on that silly hat and shot himself).

1996

Cuba Gooding Jr. wins Best Supporting Actor. This one should make up for every snub of every black performer in Oscars history. Show me the money! How about I show you my balls instead? Figures that the four Best Supporting awards ever going to blacks has one playing a slave, one playing a loud athlete, one playing an ex-boxer, and one playing a loud Air Force sergeant (1982, Lou Gossett Jr. in *An Officer and a Gentleman*, you racist). In 1985, Gossett played an alien in *Enemy Mine*, in which he spoke like he was gargling buttermilk and semen. This is a case where a film was so awful, the Academy should have gone to the actor's house, taken his previously won Oscar, and bludgeoned him to death with it.

1998

Shakespeare in Love wins Best Picture over *Saving Private Ryan*. Just kill yourselves already.

1999

Once again, those poofs at the Academy reward someone who reminds them of themselves. Kevin Spacey, Best Actor for *American Beauty* over Denzel Washington in *The Hurricane*? They reward a boring middle-of-the-road wimp over Denzel's portrayal of a falsely imprisoned inmate slowly losing his mind. This one made me want to shit in my hand and eat it (which I did, in protest).

2001

The year of the Black Oscar. For the first time in history, Best Actor and Best Actress went to black performers. First, Denzel for *Training Day*. (An Oscar that belonged to Russell Crowe for *A Beautiful Mind*.) *Training Day* was a one-level performance, like *Scarface*. It was fun to watch, but *Hurricane* blew it away. Apparently a corrupt cop is a fairly safe black Oscar bet.

Halle Berry was great in *Monster's Ball*. She played a single mom with a Fat Albert–looking kid who takes a dirt nap after a car plows into him.

Then Billy Bob Thornton fucks the dogshit out of her. And that's why she was given an Oscar; for all the moaning she did while this gangly idiot mashed his groin into hers. It took every ounce of her professional training to not laugh in his face, cry, and then vomit all over the life-size Angelina Jolie tattoo covering his entire body.

2004

A weird year. There have been worse, but some shitty decisions were certainly made:

Best Actor: Jamie Foxx for *Ray*. He was great, although pretty much just doing an impression. (Jamie was also nominated for Best Supporting Actor in *Collateral*, although no one will tell me why.) For Best Actor, I liked Don Cheadle in *Hotel Rwanda*, which was a lighthearted musical romp about genocide. He should have won.

Best Supporting Actor: Morgan Freeman, for his mundane, average performance in *Million Dollar Baby*. Jesus Christ, enough already. How about a little balance? You suddenly turned the Oscars from the John Birch Society into the BET Awards. Alan Alda deserved Best Supporting Actor for *The Aviator*. I'm tired of white people being passed over!

I'm sure that some other idiotic decisions were made in following years, but I'm even boring myself at this point. You get where I'm going. You probably got it five pages ago, yet I continued my incessant belaboring of the issue. I'm sure a lot of people will disagree with many of my picks. Nothing wrong with that. There's also nothing wrong with you disagreeing, and then promptly suffering third-degree burns on your face thanks to a grease fire. And I realize I harped on the racial angle quite a bit, but you can't deny that things have been more lopsided than Fiona Apple riding a seesaw with Rosie O'Donnell. There have been eighty Academy Award shows, and normally each category has five nominees.

Let's do a quick breakdown, so I don't get too many emails from any of you ultraconservative asshats. These are the approximate totals of nominees:

TOTAL BEST ACTOR NOMINEES: 400
BLACK BEST ACTOR NOMINEES: 17
BLACK BEST ACTOR WINNERS: 4

TOTAL BEST ACTRESS NOMINEES: 400
BLACK BEST ACTRESS NOMINEES: 7
BLACK BEST ACTRESS WINNERS: 1

TOTAL BEST SUPPORTING ACTOR NOMINEES: 400
BLACK BEST SUPPORTING ACTOR NOMINEES: 16
BLACK BEST SUPPORTING ACTOR WINNERS: 4

TOTAL BEST SUPPORTING ACTRESS NOMINEES: 400
BLACK BEST SUPPORTING ACTRESS NOMINEES: 15
BLACK BEST SUPPORTING ACTRESS WINNERS: 3

TOTAL BEST DIRECTOR NOMINEES: 400
BLACK BEST DIRECTOR NOMINEES: 1
BLACK BEST DIRECTOR WINNERS: You're kidding, right? 0

If you can't see or acknowledge any bias whatsoever here, then you (as well as the Academy of Motion Picture Arts and Sciences) can suck my big black dick.

I Hate Your Guts

IN ORDER TO BECOME A BIT MORE SOCIALLY RELEVANT, THE ACADEMY NEEDS TO DO A FEW MINOR THINGS:

- Only allow the presenters to engage in "funny banter" with each other if they're doing lines from *Raging Bull.*
- Give the Best Picture nod to "2 Girls 1 Cup."
- Every time Sean Penn says something self-righteous and predictably liberal, allow audience members to throw D cell batteries at him.
- Present Steve Martin with a Lifetime Achievement Award, and only show clips of the original comedies he has redone and ruined.
- As an act of contrition to African Americans, hire Louis Farrakhan as a host.
- Wheel Robert Redford out on a hand truck and let Martin Scorsese kick him in the balls.
- When actors talk too long, give them the "wrap it up" signal by firing cow shit at them with a paintball gun.
- Make actresses accept their trophies by squatting and picking them up with their pussy lips.
- Any actor who wins for playing a retard has to make his acceptance speech in the retard voice and then shit his pants while stupidly waddling off the stage.

Book Ideas I'm Currently Working On

SINCE THERE were unforeseen issues with *Happy Endings*, I've become slightly more gun-shy in my writing. I'm fairly sure the main objection to my collection of cunt, fart, and shit stories was the graphic language and sexual descriptions. I've vowed to make my next works profanity- and sexual innuendo–free.

- *Himmler's Whimsy*. A romantic novel set in war-torn Germany that focuses on the idiosyncratic, off-the-wall sense of humor of the oft-misunderstood Heinrich Himmler. The consummate practical joker, he once had four hundred cases of rubber dog doody shipped to his men stationed at Dachau and Auschwitz to pick up sagging morale.

- *Tap Dancing Sucks: The Gregory Hines Story*. Chronicles, through interviews and anecdotes found scrawled in men's rooms, the mid-teenage years of the dead and not-at-all missed tap dancer. Includes never before seen or cared about photos of a young, wide-eyed Gregory doing a little soft-shoe outside a Sunoco station in Memphis.

- *A Hat for Jack.* An in-depth forensic examination into the theory that John F. Kennedy would have survived his assassination attempt had he been wearing the Liberty Bell as a hat.

- *The Songs of My Father.* An alphabetical list of songs my father would croon while either in the shower or clogging the toilet. (Or, during worst-case scenarios, shitting in the shower and clogging the drain.)

- *Harry's Finch.* A touching memoir of a serial arsonist's relationship to the bird he stole from an apartment he was burning a family to death in.

- *For You, Madge.* The true story of a mentally challenged man who won the affections of the girl of his dreams by sculpting her a walrus from the white gunk that had collected on the back of his tongue.

- *A Life Owed to Solitaire.* A novella set in 1800s Italy about a large-hipped woman who avoids a gang rape by convincing her attackers to play cards instead.

Hillary "Fat Calves" Clinton

IF YOU put a gun to my head, I probably still couldn't tell you exactly what it is that makes me hate Hillary as much as I do. My reasons seem to be primarily shallow and superficial, not about the issues as much as her personally. I don't like the way she looks and I don't like the way she sounds. I am not a fan of some of her policies, but they bother me far less than her exterior.

Physical Attributes

- Her face reminds me of a puppet, minus the warmth and charisma. She has very pronounced cheekbones, which makes her face appear as if it has an ass in the middle of it. Under each ass/face cheek, she has a line running down to her chin, framing her mouth. These attributes only serve to highlight her giant choppers. When she talks, it looks as though her head is being worked by a mysterious hand that's been rammed up her turd cutter. You'll notice that when Bill is next to her, he never drinks water when she's speaking. (If you're on a scavenger hunt and need a lazy, hacky ventriloquist joke, congratulations!)

Ole Puppet Face flashing that sexy smile, seen here with James Spader.

- The title of this chapter was no accident, ladies and germs. Hillary has elephantitis of the ankles and freakishly fat calves; the combination of these two atrocities is commonly called "cankles" and causes a woman to have the fuckability of a baboon anus. The only people who should have calves this fat are bodybuilders and Russian men who carry safes uphill for a living. Fat, ham-hocky calves wrapped around my back equals minuscule, wilted cock.

- She wears orange-colored pantsuits with padded shoulders. They look even sexier with her stick-of-butter legs mushed into them. Outfits like this remind me of my grandmother, who wasn't qualified to leave the house without diapers, much less run the country. Hillary should walk around in public the way she does at home; wearing a strap-on. (At least that's how I picture her walking around when I jerk off.)

- When she smiles, she looks like Mr. Ed after a facelift.

- Her hair reminds me of different people in almost every photo I see of her. These are a few that have come to mind recently:

  - Phil Spector with a frosted mullet
  - Jon Bon Jovi in 1986
  - Ozzy on the *Ultimate Sin* tour
  - Roy Horn
  - Rod Stewart in the "Da Ya Think I'm Sexy?" video

Personality Flaws

- I have no faith in her ability to protect the country's borders when she couldn't even keep a fatty out of her bedroom. It stands to reason that her perception skills are lacking if she didn't notice lipstick on Bill's collar, or that his cock smelled like mocha-fudge gelato (an excellent indicator that your husband has either been blown by a fat girl or a six-year-old).

- She can't decide what team she likes. She claims to be a Cubs fan, but she showed up in New York City with a shitty pristine Yankees hat on her head that I wanted to remove with a flaming arrow. Then in another photo, she's wearing a Mets hat. What an out-of-touch, stupid female politician:

"I know what I'll do. I'll wear the hat of a local sports team and endear myself to the men in that city!" Fucking asshole. You want to endear yourself to the men of a city? Show up with a black eye and announce that "Sometimes, even a senator lets the supper get cold."

• She hyphenated Rodham-Clinton as a phony display of feminine independence, but I think that just made her look like a pompous Cunt-Face.

• She's a white woman of privilege, yet the second she gets up in front of black people she sounds like Kizzy from *Roots*. It's bad enough when a white teenager fraudulently adopts a black accent to assimilate; it's disgusting when it's done by someone bent on leading the free world.

• Taking a jab at Republicans, on Martin Luther King Jr.'s birthday, she said, "When you look at the way the House of Representatives has been run, it has been run like a plantation and you know what I'm talking about. . . ." It's not the statement itself that bothers me, as I think plantation references are always funny; however, the fact that she said it in the same shitty, phony urban accent is monumentally irritating. The next time she's scheduled to speak in front of a black congregation, she should just rub charcoal on her face and sing "Minnie the Moocher."

• When attempting to transform from boring woman to powerful speaker, her voice gets louder and takes on a clipped, robotic quality that sounds like an automated operator:

I . . . want . . . healthcare . . . for . . . all . . . Americans . . . and . . . the . . . number . . . you . . . have . . . reached . . . two . . . one . . . two . . . Very few things in life are as painful or embarrassing as watching someone attempt to be powerful and meaningful when they speak. Her diction implies that people should be rising up in support, but instead I want to do a headstand and diarrhea-shit into my own mouth. Stop trying to be motivational, stupid. You sound like Katharine Hepburn having a stroke.

• And enough with the fucking crying, already. It doesn't instill confidence in voters when you come off like a menopausal psychopath. I don't want to watch my commander in chief dabbing at her eyes with a Kleenex every three minutes. Hey, are you the leader of the free world or my fat aunt at a wedding? Get a hold of yourself, for Christ's sake. Rein in your emotions; you're making everyone uncomfortable. You watch her once and she's black, the next time you see her she's robot-voice lady, and the time after that she has the demeanor of a bipolar widow on Christmas morning. What's the matter, don't you know what you want to be when you grow up? Pick a fucking personality and stick with it already.

• She also wrote a book called *It Takes a Village: And Other Lessons Children Teach Us*. I hate forced, pseudoheartwarmy dreck like this. Children don't teach us a goddamn thing, except how not to kill something smaller than us when it's crying on an airplane. Without adults, children would spend their whole lives shitting their pants and swimming

Employing a gentle, engaging look. I can't tell if she's about to break into tears or a rendition of "Ziggy Stardust."

five minutes after they eat. How about *It Takes Two Parents and Perhaps a Nonmolesting Relative?* If it really takes a village, does that mean we're all allowed to spank the little douchebag? And if it's a girl and she's attractive, do all of the villagers get blow jobs when she turns eighteen (or younger, of course, if the law in your state allows)? Implying that children teach us anything is only done to bond with other idiots who couldn't keep their legs closed.

- Her husband can't even stand her. Whenever he talks about her politically, he does so with the same zeal that Britney Spears had when introducing K-Fed at the Teen Choice Awards.

- Trying to come off like a blue-collar ironworker, this fraud had to announce her pick in the 2008 Kentucky Derby. She picked Eight Belles to win, place, and show. Eight Belles came in second to Big Brown, crossing the finish line with two broken front ankles. She had to be euthanized on the track. How ironic: that's just how the Democratic primary worked out.

- Her laugh has the gentle ring of an air-raid siren. That disingenuous, horrid cackle she forces out makes her sound like a guffawing retard. One of her campaign managers probably told her that in interviews she comes off like a dykey Auschwitz guard, so she studies people's laughs and pretends she can do it too. Because that's exactly what she sounds like: some wig-wearing alien that has landed and re-created the sounds of Homo sapiens experiencing mirth. She'd sound more sincere if she slapped her knee and enunciated, "Har-har-har-dee-har-har!" It's thoroughly annoying that she thinks flashing her stupid Howdy Doody teeth and laughing out of context is somehow charming and relatable. It isn't.

- In yet another attempt to win over blue-collar workers, this time in Pennsylvania, she was filmed standing at a bar doing whiskey shots and throwing back beers like she was co-starring in *The Deer Hunter*. You want to come off like a real drinker, toots? Try doing what real drinkers do: get thrown out of the bar, puke on your pantsuit, then drive home doing eighty with your hand over one eye.

- The Bosnia lie. This psychotic bitch actually stood at a microphone and tried to come off like a World War II veteran. She claimed to have landed under heavy sniper fire, ducked for cover, and barely gotten out with her life intact. What a complete fucking dummy. She lied for no discernible reason whatsoever. How did she think no one would notice? It wasn't exactly the War of 1812, shithead—you were doing a gig with Sinbad. Her big explanation when she got called out was, "Oh, I misspoke." How is that the end of the explanation? Being busted in such an embarrassing lie, she should have announced, "I'm a psychotic asshole, and you'll never hear from me again."

- Hillary is a selfish horse's ass who refused to accept she wasn't going to get the Democratic nomination. She became such an eyesore by hanging around and refusing to go away. She should have changed her name to Herpes Clinton. Beat it, bitch, you lost.

Policies

- She cosponsored legislation to support National Airborne Day. This would have been a very acceptable bit of legislation if she'd agreed to celebrate it by jumping out of a helicopter like Omar in *Scarface*.

- She announced the launch of the New York Partnership for a Green Afghanistan. This would help revitalize Afghanistan's orchards by planting eighty thousand trees. What a wonderful way to handle the country that hosted Bin-Laden while he plotted and carried out 9/11—help assist with their gardening. And the more trees we plant, the more Americans that can be hanged by the Taliban now that they're back in power. You fucking idiot. You're a New

York senator, how about planting some trees in New York? And if you want to replace something in Afghanistan, you might want to start with clitorises and severed heads.

- She thinks the government should put five thousand dollars into a college fund for every baby born in the United States (approximately four million a year), regardless of the parents' income. This would come to $20 billion annually for a bunch of little burdens who may or may not use it for college. The plan would be a little easier to live with if it automatically excluded babies born rich or retarded.

- She wants health care for all Americans, which I agree with (except for Americans with small tits or harelips—they should get nothing but medical bills and ridicule). It's such an important issue to voters, even Republicans have started with plans for universal health care. Their plans differ slightly: Hillary wants it to be mandatory that employers contribute to their employees' insurance, whereas Republicans will hand you a map and suggest a European shithole where you might relocate to have those tonsils taken care of.

You'll notice there are far more attacks on Hillary's appearance and personality than on her policies. And there is a reason for that—I am a shallow, ill-informed clod and a lazy researcher. A lot of her policies that I read while researching her honestly weren't that bad. I may have even voted for her if she had a nicer ass.

POSSIBLE CAMPAIGN STRATEGIES FOR YOUR NEXT FAILED WHITE HOUSE BID:

- Talk with that phony black inflection all the time, and at least once point to Obama and call him a punk-ass nigga.
- Have your calves and ankles shaved down like hunks of shawarma.
- When you absolutely must make a point of laughing publicly, don't fake it. Just think of something that genuinely makes you laugh, like lowering taxes or any random male having his penis cut off.
- Only wear the hat of the team you truly root for. Granted, it may be difficult to find a cap with Karl Marx or a vagina on it.
- Write your campaign slogan on those giant fucking teeth with a paint roller.
- Become an ardent Holocaust denier.
- Angrily refer to Senator Larry Craig as "that shitdick from Idaho."
- Admit you only picked Eight Belles in the Derby because she had a smaller mouth and thinner ankles.

Do the Write Thing, Bitch

EARLIER THIS morning, I had to restrain myself from punching a flight attendant in the face. My mood is shit to begin with because all of the Los Angeles to Newark flights are booked, so I'm forced to land in Cleveland and connect to LaGuardia. A major inconvenience for a man who is not only on the go, but fancy to boot. The stupid plane was already late taking off, and I needed a pen. (I had one, but it fell out of my breast pocket and into the toilet when I leaned forward to wipe piss spatter off the seat.)

So, I was effectively sans pen and very much needed one, since my therapist suggested I jot down whenever I got the urge to pointlessly masturbate, which would hopefully help to cut down on it, thereby returning some sensation to the nerve endings in my dick. (Due to years of chimplike flogging, my cock currently has about as much sensation as the ankle bone of a diabetic.) I caught myself subconsciously squeezing my shaft and balls under the blanket, which for me is the equivalent of revving the engine before a long drive.

I had two options: a) get up out of my seat and march to the front of the aircraft to masturbate in the tiny room I had just stunk up, or b) acknowledge the urge and jot it down. I opted to write it down. But, I need a pen, and I noticed the big-titted flight attendant had one clipped to the middle of her shirt between her pinchable cleavage. I asked if I could borrow it, and her response was, "For how long?" Hmmm, I don't know, let me think . . . long enough to write CUNT across your face? (Of course I didn't say that, or I'd be writing this from a jail cell with an ethnic erection in my keister.)

Honestly, though, what the kind of an aggrevating question is that? And to a first-class passenger no less. I could almost understand if I were a member of the scum brigade seated in coach, but I was flying *first-class* for Pete's sake. Sitting cross-legged in the first row of the plane implies that I've come down with a severe case of big shot–itis, and I expect to be treated as such.

If I had one ounce of improvisational skills, when she asked me for how long, I'd have shot back something clever, like, "One minute and forty-three seconds," or "at least a week." Being the feebleminded, meek asshole I am, I murmured, "Just for a second," and then excused myself to hit the bathroom so I could jerk off to thoughts of eating her ass while diddling her clit with a pen.

SO WHERE DOES THIS LEAVE US?

Is the message here "be prepared and always carry writing implements"? Or is it "don't work in the service industry if you have the personality of a pre-menstrual wolverine"? Probably neither. If I were a gambling man, I'd bet the farm that the message is, "stop abusing your dick like it's a squeeze toy and you won't need a pen, shit-for-brains."

That Slender Fellow on George Street

VENTURING OUT of North Brunswick wasn't something I did very often in my youth. A few of us would occasionally go to East Brunswick to walk through their god-awful one-story mall. (There is *nothing* worse than a one-story mall, including drunk drivers, food poisoning, and sickle cell anemia.) It was shaped like an L, with plenty of empty stores just waiting for November so they could be temporarily filled up with horrible Christmas-themed stores.

East Brunswick occasionally, South Brunswick never. South Brunswick could have disappeared in a flash flood for all I gave a turkey; I don't think I knew one person who lived there. And to the best of my knowledge, there was no ranch-style mall in which to bore myself shitless. New Brunswick was mostly black, so going there was never something we really considered as an option, unless we felt restless and wanted to kill a few hours by running for our lives. And besides, we were thirteen-year-old weenies who obviously didn't drive, so we'd have to take the bus, thereby exposing us to more black people.

One of my best friends growing up was a guy named Frank. I really don't remember why, but one afternoon he and I decided to head to George Street, which is the main street running through New Brunswick.

There were some shoe stores, department stores, and restaurants on George Street, as well as plenty of boarded-up buildings. Think East Brunswick mall, but with prostitutes and shootings. There was nothing whatsoever on George Street that would have motivated two Caucasian nerds to sit on the bus for twenty minutes. We walked around for a little while, peering into stores and unwittingly standing out like a couple of vulnerable glow-in-the-dark potential victims. We couldn't have been more robbable if we had bank bags of money on our shoulders in place of our heads. We stopped to get ice cream, since nothing helps two white kids blend into a ghetto like soft-serve vanilla with rainbow sprinkles.

My memories of that day are vague, but the one thing that stands out is Frank's awful shirt. It was the classic MY PARENTS WENT TO FLORIDA AND ALL I GOT WAS THIS LOUSY T-SHIRT! edition. (A true legend in the genre of corny completely unfunny white person clothing jokes.) Pointy white hats with eyeholes would have caused us to stand out less.

Inevitably, we were approached by a black kid. He was probably sixteen and started asking us where we were from. "None of your fucking business, jerk-off," would have been the appropriate response instead of "North Brunswick . . . where are you from?" He politely informed us he was from New Brunswick and then asked if we had any money. Not only did we say yes, we told him how much we had (maybe twenty-five bucks between us). He asked if he could see it. Internally, this raised a red flag. Being street savvy, we knew there was technically no reason he needed to see U.S. currency, since he lived in this country and had undoubtedly seen it before. He promised he wouldn't take it, so we fished our hands into our shorts and both pulled out our money and handed it to him. You know—so he could see it. What a couple of pale-faced idiots; we just fucking handed him our money. In one motion, he took the cash and slid it into his pocket.

I Hate Your Guts

I was shocked when our tough-guy mantra of "C'mon, give it back" didn't work. He told us to leave because he had friends around the corner and they didn't like white people from North Brunswick (and the more I examine my life, the more I agree with them). We then tried the "We'll get in trouble if we don't come home with our money" angle, which has never caused a thief to change his mind, ever. After about thirty seconds, he grew sick of our girlish pleading and told us to get lost or he'd get his friends. Frank and I unanimously decided the best course of action would be to tuck our dicks back between our legs, curtsy, and Buffalo shuffle back to the bus.

The most embarrassing aspect of this scenario (besides the two-on-one advantage we failed to exploit) was that this kid was about 6'1" and couldn't have weighed more than 140 pounds. He probably didn't even live in New Brunswick; he was probably a Kenyan who stopped off to take a dump while running the New York City marathon. If I'd have encountered him ten years later, I'd have requested he not bleed or ejaculate on me.

I'd love to tell you that to this day, I'm amazed at what fairies we acted like. But I can't. I'm not even slightly amazed. Neither of us had ever been robbed, or even knew anyone who had. Technically, I don't even know if we were that day. "Let me see your money" and "Okay, here" doesn't exactly translate into a blitzkrieg-style carjacking. I was definitely a world-class pussbag at that age, but Frank honestly wasn't. He was actually a really strong guy who lifted weights and had a left jab that could inflict Down syndrome. He was a huge *Rocky* fan, would take Polaroids of the movies when they were on Showtime, and work out to that shitty theme music. That day in New Brunswick, he unfortunately panicked a bit; instead of throwing a Rocky Balboa roundhouse, he grabbed his stomach like a pregnant Adrian and collapsed onto a bag of pet food.

Jim Norton

IF MY FRIEND AND I ARE TO
RECLAIM OUR DIGNITY, YOU MUST:

- Rob Frank and I once again in that exact spot, only this time allow us to keep our self-respect by doing something more menacing, like waving a daffodil at us.
- Introduce yourself to Frank as Apollo Creed, then stick your chin out so he can break your fucking jaw.
- Bring us to a party with all of your friends, so we can begin mending fences between them and the residents of North Brunswick.
- Allow yourself to get caught raping a white woman in Broward County while wearing a shirt that says MY PARENTS WENT TO FLORIDA AND ALL I GOT WAS THIS LOUSY T-SHIRT!

Yankee Announcer John Sterling Should Be Arrested for Auditory Rape

NOTHING, AND I mean nothing, will test a Yankee fan's dedication like listening to the play-by-play announcing of John Sterling. He's been the Yankees' lead radio broadcaster since 1989, and you tend to develop a love-hate relationship with him. To be honest, I love the way he calls a game, I think he's interesting and compelling to listen to. On the flip side, his banter is absolutely riddled with catchphrases, all of which make my skin crawl. They are *horrible*. The first one I noticed was when the Yankees won a game, he'd scream, "Ball game over! The Yankees win . . . theeeeeee Yankeeeees winnnnn!" Quite an exciting call if it's a walk-off home run in the ninth. Not quite as exciting when it's an anticlimactic 9–1 Yankee victory. It wasn't about him getting carried away with the thrill of the win; it was about him squeezing in his catchphrase.

Then there are his home run calls. I always remember them being a bit schmaltzy but tolerable: *"It is high . . . it is far . . . it is . . . gone!"* He'd say this regardless of whether it was high and far, or whether it was a line drive that bounced off the right fielder's temple and cleared the fence by two inches. That said, every annoying baseball announcer has his own home run call, and at least Sterling's wasn't boring. But then it morphed, and his inflection changed, and he needlessly and annoyingly dragged out every word: *"Mmmmnnnnitttt is high, mmmmnnniittt is far, mmmnnniiit iiiissss . . . gahhhhhnnnn!"* Obviously a heinous sound. I found myself rooting for the Yanks to ground into double plays just so I didn't have to hear that drivel. I would actually like him if he didn't do his stupid home run calls and that three-minute *"Yaaannkkkkkeessss wiiiiiinnnn"* at the game's end. (Unless the other team wins, in which case he now drags out their name, which is somehow even more despicable.) Oh, and another habit he has to break is when two consecutive players hit home runs, he idiotically bellows, *"A back to back, and a belly to belly!"* Did two guys just hit baseballs over the fence, or are you describing the traveling conditions on the *Amistad*?

What's even worse than the home run call and game-winning yodel is the little catchphrases he uses for every player. These are his worse crimes of all. I would love to know what complete jackass in the Yankee front office told him this is entertaining. Here are a few of his most atrocious offenses:

Alex Rodriguez

An AAAAAAAA-Bomb, for AAAAAAAA-Rod!

This is obviously an awful call, but since it mentions nuclear weapons that were actually dropped on civilians, I can almost forgive it.

How A-Rodian!

A-Rodian is not a word, you asshol-ian.

And, of course, my personal favorite:

Alexander the Great conquers again!

Too bad his name isn't Idi or Adolph Rodriguez: the historical references would be hilarious.

I Hate Your Guts

Robinson Cano

Robbie Cano! Don't you know?

Don't we know what, John? That you're a douche? You bet we do.

Cano can do!

The fact that this is a play on the phrase "no can do" is infuriating because it accomplishes sucking and being confusing at the same time.

Hideki Matsui

A thrilla by Godzilla!

Another one I can live with, simply because he's mentioning a fictional lizard who has repeatedly destroyed Japan. I'd enjoy it even more if he mentioned other adorable aspects of Japanese culture, like daily pseudorapes by businessmen on the subways, or porn that pixilates pubic hair yet shows a woman in a wedding dress having her mouth shit in.

An upperdecky by Hideki!

This one rhymes, which makes me even more inclined to strangle John with his tie. And it almost sounds like "upper decker," which is the term used to describe shitting in someone's septic tank instead of the toilet.

Johnny Damon

Positively Damonic!

This wouldn't be nearly as horrendous if his name was Johnny Demon. But it's not.

Johnny on the spot!

I like this one simply because Johnny on the Spot is the name of a New Jersey–based company that specializes in portable toilets. Perfect, because this call is shit.

A Damonic dinger by Johnny Damon!

For a moment I was worried we were going to languish around toilets all day, but thankfully he's rushed us right back to the demon theme. And this time with three D words. Really rolls right off the tongue.

Jorge Posada

Jorgie juiced one!

Total idiocy. I don't even know what this one means. Did he squeeze the ball over a cup and make a vegetable drink out of it? Or perhaps he injected it with steroids? If he's only using "juiced" because it starts with the letter J, how about, "Jorgie Jewed one" or "Jorgie jerked one off."

Derek Jeter

Captain clutch!

I'm sure he uses this one even if Jeter hits a solo shot in the seventh when the Yankees are up 14–2. How about Captain crotch, because he's such a dick?

Melky Cabrera

The Melk man delivers!

I cannot think of anything to write that will make this one any more god-awful than it already is.

Do it the Melky way!

Yet another play on the word "milk." Which reminds me—I need to call a good massage therapist to have a load Melked out of my dick.

Jason Giambi

The Giambino!

Of course Babe Ruth was the Bambino, so it's only natural that seventy-five years later Sterling shoehorns another player's name to fit the same nickname. Now if he could only shoehorn Lou Gehrig's motor neurons into his own brain and spinal cord.

And now for a few of the older catchphrases, which were equally abysmal.

Bernie Williams

Beerrrrn, baby, Beeerrrn!

I would love this one if it were directed at a player whose lips, ears, and eyelids were lost in a flash fire.

Bernie goes boom!

This may be the one I hate most of all. Whenever I'd hear it, it would make me think Bernie was five and had just shit his pants.

Don Mattingly

Mattingly . . . Smashingly!

Mercifully, Mattingly's last season was abysmal, so we only had to endure this one seven times.

Tino Martinez

The great Bam-Tino!

Tino, of course, was the first baseman before Giambi, which makes Giambi's Babe Ruthish nickname even more revolting. It's a rip-off of a rip-off.

Shane Spencer

Shane Spencer, the home run dispenser!

This one's a winner because not only does it rhyme, it accurately describes Shane's specialty: dispensing home runs! Too bad he didn't accidentally have his throat slit while sliding into second, because then we could call him Shane Spencer, the Pez dispenser. Or would you have preferred if I cleverly mused that it was a shame he wasn't involved in the HGH scandal, so we could call him Shane Spencer, the steroid dispenser? Or a rapist—Shane Spencer, the semen dispenser! I'm giving you gold here, folks.

Robin Ventura

And Robin becomes Batman!

Too bad he didn't become Mr. Freeze. He could have cryogenically frozen Sterling's head and then shattered it into ten thousand pieces with a sidekick.

As of this writing, John is still the Yankees radio announcer, and his partner is Suzyn Waldman. Suzyn seems like a nice enough gal, but she looks like a retarded Muppet in a Lego person wig. And I hate listening to her, because she sounds like she's talking with a pinch of goose shit between her cheek and gums. She has the perfect combination for a woman; a face made for radio and a voice that isn't.

I'm sure I've overlooked some Sterlingisms. If there are any I've forgotten, feel free to MySpace them to me along with a photo of your favorite woman who is constantly being mistaken for a transsexual (see Suzyn Waldman).

TWO THINGS JOHN STERLING SHOULD BE
FORCED TO DO TO AVOID LOSING HIS JOB:

1. Only use catchphrases containing racial epithets: "An AAAAAAAA-bomb for AAAAAAAA-Spic" or "An NNNNNNNN-bomb . . ." for whichever black player hits a home run.

2. Scream "What is it, bitch?" every time Suzyn Waldman speaks.

Al Roker: Eat Like a Whale, Blog Like a Bitch

I NEVER realized it was possible to remember a weatherman's name, much less hate his guts. Since 1996, Al Roker has been the fat, jolly weatherman on the *Today* show. He seemed fairly innocuous; just a smiling, jovial yes-man whose weight made him a constant heart attack candidate. Which was the only reason I'd tune in to the *Today* show. Sitting through hours of chipper migraine-inducing banter was certainly not the only accurate way of knowing if I should grab my hat on the way out the front door. I own a computer; it takes three seconds to check local weather. I'd hope against hope that *this* was the morning Al would be clutching his fat chest, lumbering forward, and falling face first into Meredith Vieira's snatch. You'll notice that you almost never see fat people associated with news unless they're doing the weather. I guess people just look at them and assume that since they're such fatsos, their bones must ache when it's damp out, thereby making them a bit more qualified.

Writing this chapter on Roker is proving to be more challenging than I thought, simply because as I reread his blog about Don Imus, such bile is coming up in me, such venom, I truthfully don't know where to start. I don't hate Roker because of Imus; I hate Roker because he is everything I *detest*, everything I absolutely *loathe* about Americans and their perception of free speech. Especially when it comes to something said in humor *and everyone expressing outrage knows it was said in humor.*

There is this disgusting perception that they must somehow approve, or not be made uncomfortable, by something someone else says for it to be allowable. But they never come right out and say, "I don't like it, don't want to hear it, so it shouldn't be said." That's just a little too revealing a window into the self-centered, emotionally spoiled asshole saying it. So they create reasons as to why free speech doesn't cover it, reasons like "racial insensitivity" and "(insert your sacred cow here)-aphobic" or, my favorite, it's "hate speech."

And this absolutely is a free speech issue; don't let them fool you with their self-excusing garbage about how no one's rights are being taken away, employers have the right to fire you for conduct they deem inappropriate, blah blah fucking blah. If someone is paid to talk on the radio, and they say something that causes controversy, and it is NOT an FCC violation, firing them, or punishing them in any way, is attacking their free speech. I'd respect these cocksuckers so much more if they would just be honest about it.

And notice that I wrote "reread his blog." That's because like a high school girl, it's where Al goes to be truly heard. What's the matter, Malcolm X? Your "racially poignant moment" wasn't deemed appropriate for the national television show you're on? All of those years in the spotlight, and no one has ever encouraged you to "let it out," huh? It's because you're a contribute-nothing, morbidly obese hypocrite (I wanted to write that as hippo-crite so badly I could scream) whose only talent is flashing those pearly whites and keeping your tone phony and upbeat. I've gone over his blog for you, and I will quote him accurately and exactly. It begins:

> *I cannot tell you how many people have asked me about my thoughts on Don Imus.*

Allow me to venture a guess, Al . . . zero? Maybe because no one gave a shit what you thought, because it had nothing to do with you? Or, did they say, "Hey, fatso—we're going to the Imus protest tomorrow. What's the weather going to be like?"

As a student of broadcasting, I know Don Imus was one of the original "shock jocks." I listened to him growing up in New York City in the late '60s and early '70s.

Why the quotes around the words "shock jocks," you hypersensitive idiot? Jesus Christ, even in print, you're a predictable news hack.

He is a radio icon. That said, it is time for him to go. I, for one, am tired of the diatribes, the "humor" at others' expense, the cruelty that passes for "funny." Don Imus isn't the only one doing this, but today he's the one in the hot seat.

As a rule of thumb, anyone who begins a sentence with "I, for one . . ." is a pompous asshole trying desperately to sound smarter and more important than he really is. And again with the unnecessary quotes, Al? Is putting quotes around the words "humor" and "funny" your way of questioning the validity of such words? Your way of saying, "I'll write them because I understand the intent is to be humorous, but, by gum, I don't agree!" And he's the one in the hot seat? How fucking old are you, eighty? You forgot to mention other things he's in, like hot water, the doghouse, and quite a pickle.

What he said was vile and disgusting. It denigrated an entire team and by extension, a community and its pride in a group that had excelled.

Getting a little carried away there, don't you think, fat ass? "Vile and disgusting" is just a tad much. Unless of course you mean Jesse Jackson saying Hymietown, or Jesse offering tuition costs to a lying pseudoprostitute. I must have missed your angry blogs on those remarks. And I'm sure you're working on one about Jesse for wanting to take Barack Obama's testicles off and saying *nigger.* Incidentally, the "by extension, a community and its pride" didn't go far enough. You forgot to mention that after the community felt denigrated, by extension, the entire state did, which of course morphed into the entirety of the nation. The extension of agony then eased on up through Canada, hopped a British Airways flight, and began denigrating in Heathrow Airport. You get where I'm going with this, cuntface?

This controversy started and grew during the week. At first under the radar, we even had Don's wife, Deidre, on the program, talking about "green" cleaning. I thought she was so good; I wanted to talk to her about a television program for my production company.

Yawn. Oh, is that paragraph finished? Who gives a shit? The *Today* show honored a booking that they absolutely should have honored? Good for them. Why wouldn't they? Guilt by association? If that's the case, Wafa Bin Laden better stop hobnobbing like a socialite twat, and make like a tree and leave. And if you're still looking for programs for your production company, I've got an idea for a great one: it revolves around the McDonald's Grimace masquerading as a weatherman. His whole life has been one long act of gluttony, burying pain by grabbing for more than his share of food. Since he has no self-control, he decides that instead of facing the issues that cause him to eat, he'll get his stomach stapled. Unfortunately his head doesn't shrink, which actually is perfect, because now he's shaped like one of the thermometers he relies so heavily upon. Since he never dealt with what caused him to overeat in the first place, he got fat again, much to the delight of a nameless comedian. The show ends each week with the morally inconsistent blob attempting to preach on television, but the producers cut him off midsentence every time.

Don and his wife have done a lot of good things. Raising money for charity, including a ranch for children suffering from cancer and blood disorders.

This Imus sounds like a real cocksucker. Cancer *and* blood disorders? And that awful wife of his, not only aiding in this terrible charity but also attempting to make environmentally friendly products? A miracle the *Today* show would sully their airwaves with such people.

Yet, Don Imus needs to be fired for what he said. And while we're at it, his producer, Bernard McGurk, needs to be canned as well. McGurk is just as guilty, often egging Imus on.

Yet. The most infuriating thing in this entire blog is the word "yet." Don and his wife have a ranch for children with cancer, YET this fucking piece of shit wanted him fired over a joke. I can't even be funny with this one. You tunnel-visioned, self-righteous *pig*. And as far as Bernard is concerned, he's brilliant. (He does, however, look like Nosferatu, and should have been fired only if he overslept because his coffin lid wouldn't open.) And if egging on *is* a fireable offense, I guess we have to say good-bye to Matt Lauer and Ann Curry, who can be clearly heard laughing in the background when you weren't making an epilepsy joke. (Don't worry, Tubbo, I'm getting to that one.)

The hilarious Bernard McGurk, right before he leaned over and bit me on the neck.

The "I'm a good person who said a bad thing" apology doesn't cut it. At least he didn't try to weasel out of this by hiding behind alcohol or drug abuse. Still, he said it and a two-week suspension doesn't cut it. It is, at best, a slap on the wrist. A vacation. Nothing.

You're right, Al—that apology certainly doesn't cut it! (Unless of course we're talking about a fat, unfunny weatherman, in which case that apology cuts it just right, doesn't it?) And not only did Imus not attempt to weasel out of it by hiding behind substance abuse, he didn't try to weasel out of it by denying he made an epilepsy joke when he clearly did. You monumentally inconsistent scumbag.

I Hate Your Guts

The general manager of the Cartoon Network resigned after a publicity stunt went wrong and caused a panic in Boston. He did the right thing. Don Imus should do the right thing and resign. Not talk about taking a two-week suspension with dignity. I don't think Don Imus gets it.

Well then you should definitely resign, stupid. With Imus you'll throw around phrases like "repeat offender," but the Cartoon Network did some viral marketing all over the country, and no one but the dolts in Boston misunderstood it as a terrorist threat and panicked. First-time offense, and he quit. Same ought to go for you, dick. Quit and retire to Boston. Southie, to be exact.

After watching and listening to him this morning during an interview with Matt Lauer, Don Imus doesn't get it. Maybe it's being stuck in a studio for 35 years or being stuck in the 1980s. Either way, it's obvious that he needs to move on. Citing "context within a comedy show" is not an excuse.

But apparently "comedy during a weather broadcast" is an excuse. And if anybody is getting stuck anywhere, I'd venture a guess that it's you in a revolving door, you tub of blubber.

He has to take his punishment and start over. Guess what? He'll get rehired and we'll go on like nothing happened. CBS Radio and NBC News need to remove Don Imus from the airwaves. That is what needs to happen. Otherwise, it just looks like profit and ratings rule over decency and justice.

I'm sick and tired of black people overusing the word "justice." And you know what looks like profit and ratings ruling over decency and justice? The vultures in the media showing dead bodies and police tape every thirty seconds to keep viewers interested. If that's not the case, then why do they do news teases, Al? It's to keep you watching through the commercials. "Is *your* child in danger of being raped by a water buffalo? We'll tell you . . . right after these messages. . . ." For someone who accuses Imus of not getting it, *you* don't seem to get it, shitbag. The news on your very own network uses the tease of informing people about health issues and violence in order to help sell more products, so the advertising dollars keep rolling in. Sounds to me like that's placing profits over decency. Or don't you "get that," you fat fucking toad?

So ended the first blog. Everyone knows what happened next. The next day, or maybe it was even that day, Asshole Al just had to blog again. I can't remember a case of a guy trying so hard to get attention by marrying himself to a story that had nothing to do with him. And it didn't. He wrote this (and I've once again interjected my opinion and some light-hearted humor).

> *There is no joy in what has transpired over the last week. From the utterance of those foul, vile words to the dropping of Don Imus's program on MSNBC, this has been extremely difficult.*

Once again, the melodrama over the words "nappy-headed hos." You phony skunk. And what was so difficult about it: Did your sausage fingers get sore from blogging so much? Or did your big fat ass get stuck in your chair and require the fire department to come and rescue you like a clumsy rhino that has meandered into a sinkhole?

> *As someone who called for the dropping of his show, I take no personal satisfaction in the Imus program's removal.*

Another lie. Of course you do. If I called for something to be canceled, and it was, I'd feel great about it. Can you be honest about anything concerning this situation, instead of overly dramatizing it like it's the Medgar Evers case? Imus made a black joke, it was funny, you didn't like it, now go fuck yourself.

I am proud of the courage our president of NBC News, Steve Capus, has shown in making this difficult decision. I'm gratified by the hundreds of emails I've received thanking me for my stance. And I appreciate the other hundreds of emails I got that were less than complimentary. Why?

First of all, what courage shown by Steve Capus? As soon as Jesse Jackson and Al Sharpton showed up, he threw his goddamn hands up in the air faster than the Kuwaiti army. And how difficult was it really, Al? He was afraid of losing cash due to the threat of boycotts. And what is it with guys like you and Olbermann lapping your bosses' asses? Holy moly, are you a couple of gutless, safe-stance-taking soccer moms.

A line has to be drawn as to what is acceptable and what will not be tolerated. A dialogue has been started about race in our country. An opportunity has been created to start holding responsible those who produce and broadcast offensive music lyrics, both rap and rock, that denigrate and marginalize women.

What dialogue, Al? The one where black people have proven how they're very comfortable with a double standard in the language? I know how awful America's racial history is, so why don't blacks just admit they want that language double standard and are comfortable with it? A dialogue about race? Fuck you. Even rappers wanted Imus yanked. Nice to know that the first chance they got, hardcore thugs reacted like suburban white women. And as far as holding people responsible, who the hell do you think you are? Don't you realize, you absolute dummy, that what society deems offensive is a transient thing, that what is offensive today wasn't yesterday, and so on? Maybe we shouldn't positively acknowledge interracial relationships because they offend a certain segment of the population, huh? You're a cookie-cutter, thought-police liberal douchebag. I hope you get your ashy scrotum caught on a glue trap.

We can use this time to look at ourselves and dig deep to create a world that our children will be proud to inherit. Diversity, inclusion, and acceptance are great goals to strive for.

And you know what else is a great goal to strive for? Defending speech we find offensive, being it's one of the bedrock principles of the Constitution, you vomit bag with teeth. And incidently, what children are you referring to? The ones with cancer and blood disorders that Imus was raising money for when he was fired in the middle of a charity radiothon? Are those the kids you're referring to? Figures you'd have to play the children card during this whole thing: "Waiter, I'll have another cliché, please!"

For all those who think this punishment is too harsh, consider having to explain to your daughter why someone would call a person they didn't know a "nappy-headed ho."

I can't consider it because instead of having a daughter, I've chosen to blast my loads on women's faces, backs, and foot arches. But if you've *chosen* to have a kid, then part of parenting, you four-eyed sack of turtle shit, is explaining things to them. And in a world where ethnic cleansing is prevalent and 9/11 is still a fresh memory, if your idiotic kid actually asked why the bad man said that mean thing to the nice people, then your kid is the mental equivalent of a catfish, and you should address your wife's boozing during pregnancy and leave Imus out of it. And if you must explain it, show them a photo of the girl's hair and open a dictionary to the word "nappy." . . .

And by the way, for all those people who posit the phrase is rooted in the black community, it is not. My childhood community of St. Albans, Queens, is a middle-class neighborhood. People keep their homes neat and their lawns mowed. I never heard the word "ho" in my neighborhood or in my parents' house. To this day, when I go back to take my kids to see their grandmother, there aren't young black men on the corner calling women "hos."

You're right. "Nappy-headed hos" is exactly how white people would say it. Good point, Al. We all know, from our day-to-day experiences in life, that's exactly how white people speak. Sounds to me like someone has a case of the "successful black man guilties" and is trying desperately to be more closely associated with color-related issues in the black community. I probably would be too, if I spent every morning running around with a bunch of white people and entertaining a predominately white audience. And by the way, balloon face, if everyone in your neighborhood had such immaculate lawns, how did you never hear the word "hoe"? What did they do all of their gardening and weeding with, their big pointy dicks?

In the end, this is not about Don Imus or his producer, Bernard McGurk, who often set the ugly and hateful tone of the "comedy" bits they produced.

Someone's getting quote happy again. . . .

The ten young women of the Rutgers women's basketball team showed how unjust and wrong the humor of the Imus program is.

How did they do that? They didn't even win the fucking game. I've had enough of these broads being painted as Nobel Peace Prize winners. I'm sure they're absolute saints, but they were throwing a ball through a goddamn hoop, not curing juvenile diabetes.

Mr. Imus says he's a good person who said a bad thing. That may be true. Certainly his charity work speaks to that. But just as he wants to be judged on what he does, he must also be judged on what he says and what he has said, both on and off the air.

You put the millions of dollars he raises for sick children in the backseat to a joke you objected to about a bunch of chicks pretending to be Meadowlark Lemmon? I not only hope you get completely fat again, but I also hope your stomach staples are blown off and shit spews all over your slacks and shoes.

Mr. McGurk contends he's not a racist, even though he spews racist invective because, in his words, he grew up around black people. Hmmm, so did Strom Thurmond.

What was the "Hmmm" for? Was that written intentionally, or was it just you deciding between living long enough to see your kids grow up or indulging yourself with another slice of blueberry pie?

I Hate Your Guts

Thursday, June 7, 2007
(Less Than Two Months After Imus Was Fired)

A lot of controversy had been surrounding the proposed logo for the 2012 Olympics in London. There was something about the way it flashed that triggered something in epileptics' brains, that, in turn, triggered seizures. This alone was reason enough to not only keep the logo but also use it for every other product on the market. No matter how down in the dumps you were feeling, you could always take a quick walk to the supermarket and watch epileptics making assholes out of themselves in the aisles.

I guess they were taking some sort of cheesy poll on the *Today* show about it, and gave the segment to Al since no real skill would be involved. Well, "comedian" that he is (using quotes for no reason is empowering and fun, I see his point!), Al decides to make a little jokey-poo:

> *Remember that controversial Olympic logo for the 2012 Olympics in London? Some folks have complained that the campaign actually sent them into epileptic seizures. Well, we asked you to weigh in on our website in an informal poll; those of you who could get up off the floor after shaking around were able to actually log in. . . .*

When I heard this, of course I was thrilled that this brontosaurus had stuck his hoof in his mouth. Under any other circumstances, I would have laughed, as it's not a bad joke. Being a nation of petulant crybabies, of course there was "outrage" and a "firestorm" over his "inappropriate remark." I was also thrilled that he wasn't nearly as "sick of humor at others' expense" as he mused on his blog. He really didn't do anything wrong, although I was hoping for him to not only be fired, but executed with a petrified horse cock. The next day, he did what we all knew he'd do . . . he lied.

> *I started joking about it. I want to make this clear—I was not joking about epilepsy or anyone who suffers from epilepsy.*

Yes, you were. Truth be told, you were joking about epilepsy AND people who suffer from it. As you should have been. And if you had any real balls, you'd have used the epilepsy joke to segue nicely into a Parkinson's rant.

> *We understand and know that this is a serous affliction and would never joke about that.*

What's this *we* shit? That was a *you* joke, not a *we* joke. All Matt and Ann did was laugh at it and egg you on. And as far as never joking about it, you did so on yesterday's show. . . .

> *We were joking about the logo—not about epilepsy. If anybody was offended, I heartily and really humbly apologize.*

Not good enough! Off with his fat head! See how easy it is to offend people? I just hate the fact that he lied through his overused teeth. How is getting up off the floor after shaking around, in reference to a logo causing epilepsy, not an epilepsy joke? If that's the case, here's a hilarious bird joke you can tell on the *Today* show: A black man walks into a room with a giant multicolored parrot on his shoulder. Someone says to him, "Hey, that's a weird-looking animal. Where'd you get it?" and the parrot says, "Africa." HAHAHAHA, get it?? The joke is about the bird, and how he can not only talk but also has trouble differentiating human beings from other animals. HAHAHA. And the guy wasn't even from Africa, he was from Detroit! HAHAHAHA, that stupid bird!

Al Roker didn't suffer any consequences whatsoever, simply because the left-wing scumbags at Media Matters didn't go after him for it, and for a couple of reasons:

1. He's black.

2. Epileptics aren't sacred cows of left-wing ideology.

3. He's black.

I may as well wrap this one up, lest I reiterate my points a fiftieth time. Imus, hypocrite, Imus, epileptic, hypocrite, Imus—we get it, Jim, we get it. At the end of the day, Imus sat for a while and was rehired within the year. Al Roker was kicked off his high horse and put back down where he belongs: just another meaningless weatherman with a blowhole. Or Raj's mother from *What's Happening!!* Let's take a quick tally to close this chapter about Al, shall we?

SALIENT POINTS: 3
GRATUITOUS REFERENCES TO AL'S WEIGHT: 29

You may be asking yourself, "Jim, other than pulling his cock out on television and slapping Meredith Vieira's face with it, is there anything this hypocritical plankton-eater can do to redeem himself?" My answer to you would be, "Indeed there is! Al would be A-OK in my book if he were to bring an epileptic on the *Today* show, hand him a full pot of

When all is said and done, I had my shot to really trash him to his face. What did I do? Smiled, took a picture, and snuck home to peck-peck-peck away at my keyboard like a faggot. I make myself sick.

coffee, and apologize as the epileptic clumsily scalded his wrists and forearms with the piping-hot beverage." Or, how about just an accurate weather report every once in a while? What process does this dunce go through to come up with his predictions, finger a cow as his arthritis is acting up? Look out the fucking window, once in a while, ass face.

UPDATE!!

"Plankton-eater" officially brought the gratuitous references to Al's weight up to 30.

The Rock and Roll Hall of Shit, Part One

WHAT DO KISS, Ted Nugent, Rush, Tom Jones, and Iron Maiden have in common? The answer may surprise you. Some of the most common incorrect guesses to this question are:

- They all wore makeup onstage?? No, you silly goose, only KISS did that.

- They were all born in Wales?? Incorrect, you cancerous tumor. That would only be Tom Jones (and possibly one of the forty members of Iron Maiden—my laziness prevented me from researching any further).

- They all love guns and refer to themselves as Uncle Ted?? Yup, you got it. I'm teasing you good-naturedly, of course. That would be Ted Nugent, you blithering, know-nothing cunt.

What all of these artists have in common is that none of them are in the Rock and Roll Hall of Fame. (I will assume that you knew this by the title of this chapter, and were only guessing incorrectly to jerk me off a little.) Maybe you could excuse these omissions if the R&RHoF (that's the abbreviation for Rock and Roll Hall of Fame!) had inducted only three bands: the Beatles, U2, and the Rolling Stones. But that obviously isn't the case. My HATRED of this institution began a few years ago when I realized that Black Sabbath had been rejected for induction year after year after year.

The original title of this chapter (as we all know, there is nothing more entertaining than the history of a chapter title), was "The Rock & Roll Hall of Fame Museum." I had vowed never to set foot inside of it, at least not until Sabbath was inducted (they finally were, in 2006, after a ten-year wait). I ended my boycott and saw the museum for myself a few months ago when I was in Cleveland (home of the Indians, Browns, and meatiest pussies this side of Timbuktu). I was surprisingly impressed. There was great memorabilia on display—guitars, original childhood drawings of some of the artists, historic clothing, etc. (I may even go back next year since it's rumored they'll be displaying Yoko Ono's clit and the underwear John Lennon shit into when he saw Chapman's pistol.)

Whoever it was that took me on the tour and showed me around explained that the museum itself didn't vote. That end of it is handled by the Rock and Roll Hall of Fame Foundation, based in New York. In fact, the Rock and Roll Hall of Fame is only one wing of the entire museum building. So, to hate the museum itself is like hating your ex-girlfriend's house. She's the cunt, not the building. (I came up with the brilliant ex-girlfriend/house analogy, but I stole the cunt/building joke from a *Fat Albert* episode.)

The R&RHoF was cofounded in 1983 by *Rolling Stone* founder Jann Wenner. First, and most important, *Rolling Stone* magazine is FUCK-ING BORING. My mother bought me a subscription when I was a teenager and I think I used every page of every issue to wipe a load out of my belly button. Secondly, I don't trust a man named Jann. Partially because he has a girl's name, and partially because he insists on keeping two "n"s in it. (And yes, I do realize his name is pronounced "Yahn," but I enjoyed my little joke anyway.)

According to the R&RHoF website, here's how it works: once an artist is nominated by the committee, ballots are sent out to an internal voting body of more than five hundred "rock experts," and they all vote. The nominating committee itself is a bunch of fruity music snobs who have never liked the music I like. They're critics and dull *Rolling Stone* writers whose "too hip for the room" attitude makes my balls ache. And the voting body consists of the living inductees, writers, music business people, and I'm sure some other complete idiots I'm omitting. Some of their decisions made me want to shit in my sock and swing it around in circles over my head (in an area where the voting body was gathering . . . to swing it around my own apartment would be counterproductive and silly goose–ish).

One of the criteria they look for is "the influence and significance of the artists' contributions to development and perpetuation of rock and roll." Back to Sabbath. They are credited by almost every metal band, without fail, to be the creators of the heavy metal genre. Is that not influential enough? Does creating a subgenre of rock and roll not count as the perpetuation of it? Yet they were rejected, systematically, until Ozzy finally said, "Fuck this, take us off the ballot." I'm not sure what happened, perhaps whoever was voting realized what irrelevant, dumb motherfuckers they were beginning to look like.

I do understand that musical tastes are different, and not everyone is going to love Black Sabbath (although everyone who doesn't should have their eardrums raped with a stick). But, when you see some of the other artists inducted during the years of Sabbath's eligibility, you want to smash your head through a window. Or maybe you won't. Maybe you'll just think, *Gee, that was an odd choice*, and go on with your life. A few examples of artists inducted in the years Sabbath was passed over:

- **THE BEE GEES.** An enjoyable, toe-tapping disco band. Their biggest influence was on sucking cock.

- **CARLOS SANTANA.** Fucking asshole doesn't even sing. Decent guitarist, I suppose, but most of his songs suck. Extraordinarily overrated.

- **THE EAGLES.** Mediocre, light-rock cornballs. Don't get me wrong; I enjoy *Hotel California* as much as the next asshole in his late fifties. They influenced dick.

- **FLEETWOOD MAC.** I don't care how many albums they've sold, they fucking suck.

- **BONNIE RAITT.** I'm not that familiar with her work, but I guarantee she's no Sabbath. Fuck her.

- **STEELY DAN.** Terrible. I'd rather have the radio fart in my face than play that boring shit.

- **TALKING HEADS.** New Age dreck. It's all downhill after "Psycho Killer." They should rent a bus with Devo and drive it off a fucking cliff.

- **TOM PETTY & THE HEARTBREAKERS.** Bleeeechhh, also vastly overrated. They have a few good songs, I'll give them that. But Ozzy and the boys shit in their mouths.

- **BOB SEGER.** He makes me want to "take those old records off the shelf" and break them with a croquet mallet. He's a dullard, and influences nobody to do anything. Fuck him in the ear.

- **JACKSON BROWNE.** Are they fucking kidding with this one? Horrible. A hero to the left-wing baby boomers. Another lackluster douchebag who influences people to put their head on a pillow and count sheep.

- **THE PRETENDERS.** Chrissie Hynde has a mullet, which should have been enough to automatically exclude them from eligibility. "Back on the Chain Gang" is a serviceable song. I don't love it, nor would I leap off the toilet midshit to turn it off. Most of their other work is unmemorable background music.

Allowing for differences in taste, what I find so irritating is that the Hall is so influenced by a small, very predictable group. Most of these assholes feel like they're letting their hair down if they wear jeans with their collared shirt. They've *never* embraced bands like Sabbath and KISS and Motörhead, so making theirs the primary sensibility that decides who's inducted automatically deep dicks these bands in the ass. I guarantee the Dave Matthews Band is a first year of eligibility, first ballot induction. Horrid.

The year 2008 was particularly enraging. John Mellencamp was inducted. Why?? I can name exactly two songs this flannel shirt–wearing mope has done, and both of them are average at best. As far as I'm concerned, Jack and Diane can go shit in their hats. And they inducted Madonna on her first year of eligibility. What a fucking JOKE. She's obviously good, and seems to reinvent herself every year. Fine. In the spirit of honesty, I have quite a few of her songs on my iPod. (As I wrote that, a black dick should have sprouted from my chair and perforated my colon.) But a first ballot induction on her first year of eligibility while Black Sabbath sat on the sidelines for ten years? FUCK YOU. Madonna is a pop star. She belongs on a plaque with Britney Spears and the New Kids on the Block, not Zeppelin and the Rolling Stones.

And 2007 saw R.E.M. predictably inducted on their first year of eligibility. A band like that carries the attitude that *Rolling Stone* likes: average, nonthreatening, and gay. "Losing My Religion" is alternative bubble-gum rebellion and "Everybody Hurts" makes me want to curl into a ball and suck my own hog. These 'mos are the roots of Emo music and should throw their nude bodies into a lye pit.

A recent controversy that has erupted is whether or not rappers should be included in the Hall. Grandmaster Flash & the Furious Five was inducted in 2007. Why not, and while you're at it, toss in barbershop quartets, ukulele players, and comedians who do song parodies! Hey, you people-pleasing, codependent assholes: it's the Rock and Roll Hall of Fame, keep it to people who play rock and roll. I like rap, and I like Grandmaster Flash, but who gives a shit? I also like cheesecake and transsexuals, but it doesn't mean they deserve an exhibit next to Bo Diddley.

Why doesn't the Hall just admit they are looking to get press, or entice people to hit the museum, or whatever other irritating motives they may have. "Papa Don't Preach," "Material Girl," "Vogue": first-year induction. "Paranoid," "War Pigs," "Children of the Grave": ten-year wait. "Limelight," "Red Barchetta," "Tom Sawyer": still on the outside looking in. What a fucking disgrace.

Here are a few bands, some already mentioned and some not, that the Hall should be utterly embarrassed not to have in:

- **DIO.** One of the longest-lasting, most powerful voices in heavy metal history. One of the true greats. But I wouldn't hold my breath; he's no Madonna.

- **METALLICA.** They've been eligible for two years. They'll eventually get in. Maybe they would've been inducted on their first year if the faggot voting board wasn't giving the okay to Grandmaster Flash & the Furious Five.

- **BRYAN ADAMS.** No one admits it, but we all love Bryan Adams. "Heaven," "Summer of '69," "Cuts Like a Knife":

Uncle Ted, having his photo taken with me because he thought I was the world's largest shrew.

each one more fun to sing along to than the next. Am I losing you on this one? I think I'm gay.

- **TED NUGENT.** Another guy I'm not a big fan of, but keeping him out is probably more about his politics than his music. Maybe they'd induct Ted if he promised not to shoot or fuck any wild animals for at least a year.

- **DEF LEPPARD.** I'm not a huge fan, but Jesus Christ, Rick Allen is a one-armed drummer. It would be worth inducting them just to watch him try to hold his trophy and drink a beer at the same time.

- **OZZY OSBOURNE.** He's in with Sabbath, but also deserves to be in for his solo material. Or am I just rooting for the home team and being greedy?

- **IRON MAIDEN.** How the heck (excuse my language) is this band not in that shitty Hall of Fame? Their music was heavy and original, with original themes. And Bruce Dickinson can most certainly belt out a tune. Considering Bruce's huge bulge in all the Maiden posters, I'm surprised those Tinkerbells at *Rolling Stone* didn't vote them in on the first ballot.

- **KISS.** They were the biggest things on the planet in the 1970s and never got an ounce of critical respect. If you were visiting the Hall, what would you rather see—a shitload of KISS memorabilia or that fascinating Percy Sledge exhibit?

In a limo, listening to the brand-new Motörhead CD with Lemmy, as we give our salute to the Hall of Fame.

- **MOTÖRHEAD.** They absolutely, unequivocally deserve to be inducted. There are only three of those fuckers, yet every song is balls to the walls heavy with an amazing beat. Not to mention what a brilliant songwriter Lemmy is. And he does enough speed to power a Midwestern city. They deserve to be in, but probably never will be.

Have I made my point thus far?
(To be continued in Part Two)

The Gentleman of Color from Franklin Township Who Punked Me at the Water Fountain

NORTH BRUNSWICK was a very mushy suburban town, and even the black kids who talked a lot of shit were fairly nonviolent. Whenever a kid would move in from a truly tough area, he immediately got a lot of respect. There was one such kid from Franklin, which was a couple of towns over.

I was walking up to the water fountain one afternoon when he literally shoved me out of the way and mumbled, "Punk ass," as he leaned down for a refreshing drink. People were standing around so I had to react. And I did: I stood there passively, like a fat-titted sheep, and said, "Aight . . . you got that." Reliving that memory and writing it down is so mortifying my scalp is actually tingling. "*You got that,*" like two masculine rivals had been vying for the fountain and through some stroke of good fortune it was he who wound up making it there first. "*Aight . . . you got that*" is what Larry Holmes should say to Michael Spinks after losing a fifteen-round decision, not what Reginald Denny should mumble as a toilet is being careened off his head.

If there was any God at all, camel cum would have shot up out of the fountain and he would have swallowed the unpleasant mouthful that was meant for me. (Of course, that didn't happen, or it would have been headline news and you'd have read about it.) Instead, cool, delicious water sprang forth and he probably gulped down twice as much as he would have had I not been waiting. And, of course, the friend he was with cut in front of me as well. I said nothing, as I felt it would be in poor taste to allow one man to symbolically rape me, then all of sudden try to reclaim my pride when his friend slid in for a piece of my already sore and open rump.

Historically, water fountains have been a sore spot for black people in this country, so I tried to comfort myself with thoughts of how he may have won the battle, but lost the war.

Since I've never been one to hold grudges, I have come up with the perfect scenario to even things up and allow a friendship to follow:

Very simply, this asshole, whose name I don't remember, could make everything all right if he'd allow me to cut him in a line of some sort. Perhaps we could arrange to meet discreetly on the twentieth floor of a burning building. As people are filing down the steps one after the other, he could step aside like a gentleman and allow me to enter the stairwell ahead of him. As I made my way down the stairs to safety, he could stay on the twentieth floor and try to extinguish his burning flesh by taking giant gulps of water and spitting the mouthfuls on himself.

A Few More Book Ideas

IN RESPONSE to the overwhelming popularity of the "Book Ideas I'm Currently Working On" chapter, I've decided to include a second "sneak peek" chapter. I finally settled on "A Few More Book Ideas" as a chapter title, since this is a list of a few more books I'm working on that weren't mentioned in the first chapter dedicated to this subject.

- *Kiss Me, Chip!* A hilarious short story about a boy sharing his first kiss with a drunken fifty-year-old man in the back of a van. Told from the perspective of third-grader Chip Chipperson.

- *The Diaries of Bill Mueller.* Penned in the late 1600s in Salem, Massachusetts, and recently unearthed during a septic tank dig. The depressing chronicles of air-conditioning repairman Bill Mueller, who is virtually unemployable due to chronic alcoholism, and the fact that air-conditioning is still hundreds of years away from being invented.

- *Guess What? You're Dead.* My first real crack at a murder mystery. Set on a train in London, people begin disappearing every time the train goes under a bridge or through a mountain. Vampire hunter Jacob Abromowitz not only smells a rat . . . he formulates a plan to flush that rat out in the open! But there's a catch—the killer isn't a vampire at all, but an anti-Semetic werewolf. In addition to being totally unafraid of Jacob's garlic, he is consumed with bitterness that a Jew is waving such an odoriferous culinary treat in his face.

- *Are You There God? It's Me, Terry.* Inspired by Mother Teresa's confessions about struggling with her faith, I've appropriated her writings and spiced them up with racist and homophobic language for comedic effect.

- *A Season of Hope.* Genocide and crimes against humanity are being committed throughout Darfur. See how one warlord brings a community together by organizing a fast-pitch softball league.

The Rock and Roll Hall of Shit, Part Two: The Induction of Black Sabbath

ALTHOUGH I tend to keep it under my hat, I'm slightly biased when it comes to Sabbath. And while I've had the privilege of interviewing Tony, Geezer, Bill, and Ozzy individually ("interviewed" is a stretch— held a microphone in their faces and stared like an autistic while they talked), I've never had a shot at meeting the band together. I learned of their March 13, 2006, induction around October or November 2005, and immediately began to panic. I jumped on the phone to my managers and agents, and tried to set the wheels in motion for a photo with the band. They're getting older and don't tour together as much; instinctively, I understood this may be the one true shot I'd have in my lifetime. And since the induction was taking place at the Waldorf in New York, which is literally ten minutes from my apartment, I figured I had to make a real effort. (And the Waldorf holds fond memories for me; I once had my cock sucked by Bunny Ranch hooker Isabella Soprano in one of the suites.) Everyone I asked gave a lot of lip service: "Sure, we'll get back to you" and "Yeah, definitely, we'll see what we can do," but it was obviously a lot of palaver from a bunch of disinterested show-business assholes. No one seemed to understand, or care, that I would perform fellatio on a shotgun barrel if this didn't happen.

As January rolled into February, I really began to panic, and by the time March showed up, I was in a constant state of frustration, depression, and rage. It's nice that I kept it all in perspective: I can't get an immediate yes for a photo with four Englishman, and I'm suffering on the same emotional roller coaster as the parent of a missing child. I am admittedly a spoiled, no-priority little bitch. Not one person seemed to have any interest in helping me.

Blondie was being inducted along with Sabbath, and Metallica was not only performing but also inducting Sabbath. I have the same personal-appearance agents as Blondie and Metallica *who had a table at the fucking event.* Tough titty—no dice. The only shot I had was not even going to get me in to see them inducted—a press pass that would have me stuck in the back room, away from the action, with the press. I'd be more psyched to be stuck in a bear cave with honey on my dick. And the even better news was that the only shot I had at even getting a press pass depended on Ron and Fez producer Black Earl. This was a devastating realization, as Earl doesn't have enough juice to get me a pass to a Ron and Fez event.

In the meantime, I still had a comedy career to try to balance with my sexual addiction, and I was booked by HBO to perform at the comedy festival in Aspen to promote *Lucky Louie.* The Aspen festival never had much use for me, so I was kind of glad to finally be an invited guest. I was booked to perform March 8–11, and fly home the morning of the twelfth. You may at this point be thinking, *Now, Jim, why this coma-inducing itinerary rundown?* Very simply, Aspen gets despicable snow. So I began to freak out that I'd get stuck on the twelfth, fly out late on the thirteenth, and thereby miss the induction, in which case I'd have run down the aisles of the aircraft biting people's faces. Against the advice of my managers, I canceled my big Saturday night show and flew home Saturday morning. (Good thing I did. A snowstorm rolled in and trapped everyone in Aspen's portable toilet–size airport for almost twenty-four hours. Undoubtedly, I'd have been violently arrested had I gotten stuck there.)

The induction was now less than twenty-four hours away and I was still no closer to that goddamn photo than I had been four months ago. I couldn't have slept worse on Sunday night if two crickets were fucking on the bridge of my nose. Monday morning rolled around, I walked into work bleary-eyed and almost suicidal; I had no press pass and no connection to the band. My spirits picked up a bit when I found out Bill Ward would be calling in to the show. I figured I could always hit him up for assistance on the morning of the biggest day of his life. Bill called in and is one of the nicest guys in the business, but apparently has fewer connections in the Black Sabbath organization than I do.

Shortly after, I finally got some really good news. My buddy Kevin Chiamanti, who worked for Sanctuary records, had set up a lunch for me with Tony Iommi and a couple of XM producers. Turns out Tony loves radio, and wanted to discuss doing a show on XM. So after the show we walk across the street and the next thing you know, I'm sitting at a table ordering lunch next to Tony Iommi. It was surreal. (And I only sat next to him because I hip-checked our stupid producer Steve out of the way so hard he almost crashed through the salad bar.)

Turns out I'm a better actor than I thought, because despite the pile of shit in my boxers, I was coming off as calm, cool, and collected. I wasn't. Twice I had to go into the bathroom to hyperventilate while enjoying the ass fumes of some corporate thief in a suit. We sat there for almost two hours. He and I pretty much just talked to each other while everybody else did whatever they were doing, which could have been fire breathing for all I knew or cared. We shook hands at the end, and I was actually too embarrassed to ask for any help. I hinted, but when he didn't take the bait, I decided against being Gary Greedy. Fuck it. I talked to Bill and spent almost two hours with Tony—both on the day of induction. Good enough for me. I was going to call Earl and say forget it, but on the outside chance I'd get that pass, I stopped and rented a tuxedo instead.

Of course, Earl couldn't get me a press pass. Hezbollah's TV station had a better shot of getting me one than I did through Earl. Ron Bennington luckily had a pass under his name that he wasn't going to use, so Early said he'd try to get my name on it instead. I was prepared to give up, except I had people at MTV and VH1 working on it for me too. The VH1 people couldn't do anything and they were filming the goddamn thing. I figured I wouldn't get in and I wanted to sleep—I was exhausted. Yet six o'clock that night I found myself in the back of a taxi, in a tux, headed to the Waldorf.

Unless you're completely retarded (a distinct possibility if you've purchased this book), you've probably surmised that Earl did indeed get my name on the pass. Turns out that hanging in the press area gave me the most freedom to move around, and all the bands were coming back to answer questions. Since it was all press and no fans (nameless, tuxedo-wearing undercover assholes aside), security was very relaxed. I positioned myself in the second row, armed with questions and no less than three different people, strategically placed around the room, with instructions to photograph me as I asked the band questions. This would be my shot. There were signs all over requesting PLEASE REMAIN SEATED IF YOU'RE IN THE **FIRST TWO ROWS** AS A COURTESY TO THE PHOTOGRAPHERS BEHIND YOU. Oh yeah? Fat fucking chance, Charlie. Those know-nothing assholes can take their Polaroids from the top step of a rickety ladder unless they want some fine shots of the back of my head.

I Hate Your Guts

Appearing professional, yet inwardly fighting a stroke, I sat in the second row, perfectly positioned to question the band when they walked out. And a moment later, out walked Black Sabbath; I was ten feet away from them. Tony Iommi actually recognized me and nodded and smiled when he walked out. That was all I needed. I jumped up like someone just tasered my scrotum and started in with the first question. Immediately, those deluded reporters behind me started in with, "Down in front! We can't see, sir, please have some courtesy and sit down!" Hearing these loudmouths rudely bellow while I was attempting to conduct a gentleman's interview was tempting me to stand on my chair and open my asshole up to them. Because not only was I not going to sit, but as Sab-

This shitty photo of me and the band was taken by Earl. It's a shitty photo because:

a) There are four hundred other people in it.
b) Ozzy is effectively blocking Bill Ward, so I am working this hard for a photo with three quarters of the band.
c) This idiot might as well have taken the photo from the sixth floor of the book depository.

bath answered my question I turned slightly so Earl could get a better angle on me. I figured he'd be right there, but idiot Earl decided to stand on the other side of the room. The four band members must have thought I had developed muscular dystrophy in the time I asked the question to when they answered.

I generously sat down and allowed a few of the other hundred or so people to ask a question, but their questions sucked. "Any new albums planned?" Ugggh. Horrible, predictable garbage. Sabbath deserved better. These were hacky, meaningless questions being asked to the creators of heavy metal and I wasn't going to stand for it. My four favorite people were not going to have such a monumental day in their career dulled-down by a flock of vultures who probably couldn't name two albums or a song after "Paranoid." I pretty much hijacked the press conference, asking real fan questions, about their feelings about the critics not treating them right, if being inducted was satisfying or if there was bitterness because of the long wait, etc. Sabbath addressed mostly me throughout. It

The world's greatest band speaking to the world's most irritating asshole.

got to a point where I heard a collective groan behind me every time I asked a question. Good. Groan all you want, cocksuckers, but do it quietly. I'm shooting the breeze with Ozzy, Tony, Geezer, and Bill.

After the press conference, I corralled Earl and we miraculously weaseled our way behind the curtain where the band was doing a couple of quick TV interviews. Ozzy came out first, so I asked for a photo. As we took the photo, I tried to stall to wait for the other three guys to finish up and come out. He wanted to just take the picture and leave. He wasn't being a dick—he was exhausted from a long day and slightly annoyed with my stall tactics. Not that you can tell from the photo we took.

Finally he said, I gotta go, man, you can get those guys when they come out," and began walking away. As I watched Ozzy walk down the hall, I saw this moment that I had worked so hard for, was so close to, going down the drain. My fat mouth opened and I actually whined,

Only I could manage to irritate poor Ozzy on his big day.

"Noooo," like a three-year-old girl. Moments later Tony appeared and stopped to say hello. I was fucking desperate, so I just blurted out, "Tony, I want to get a picture with the whole band and Ozzy's walking away. Can you help me? I might never get this chance again." I had, in effect, just tattled on Ozzy Osbourne for wanting to go home with his family. Tony must have really loved the Cobb salad he had for lunch that afternoon because he called to Ozzy, "Hey, Ozz, wait up a minute." So Ozzy stopped, and Tony, Geezer, and I approached. I reluctantly handed Earl my camera, but it dawned on me that I only had three of the four. We needed Bill Ward. Bill walked out in what seemed like forty minutes later to see the four of us standing like homos with our arms around one another. I panicked and yelled, "Come on, Bill, hurry up." And he does. He runs over to jump in the picture, and as he's running, I can see his expres-

The five biggest smiles in the world. (Except for Ozzy, who looks anxious to leave, and Tony, who appears to be mumbling, "Hurry the fuck up," and Bill Ward, who looks like he wants to ram his trophy up my ass for rushing him.)

sion change to "Who the fuck are you?" And then Earl—beautiful, sweet Earl—took the greatest photo of my life, commemorating the greatest moment of my life. Me, with Sabbath, all holding their Rock and Roll Hall of Fame trophies. No other fan alive has this shot.

A MERCIFULLY BRIEF SUMMATION:

In closing, I have two things to say to the Rock and Roll Hall of Fame:

1. Fuck you!

2. Thank you, for the greatest moment of my life.

And I mean both of these things from the bottom of my heart.

Myself, for the Most Pathetic Celebrity Shout-Out in History

MY EXPERIENCES with celebrities have been, for the most part, an unbalanced, slightly humiliating exercise in hero worship. They never seek me out and almost never recognize me. A few years ago, I was at an HBO party in LA, running around getting photos with people. You'd think I never set foot on a stage in my life, but rather just showed up at the party with my high school friend who did community theater. The entire cast of *Entourage* was there, as well as some guys from *The Sopranos* and *The Wire*.

I wound up walking behind Robert Iler, who played A.J. on *The Sopranos*. Being the panicky-Pete asshole I am, I drew a complete blank on his real name and blurted out, "Hi, A.J.!" This is fine if you see him unexpectedly in the Staten Island Mall. However, when you're at a talent party, and you call talent by their character names, you sound like an out-of-place hick. He responded very nicely, I'm sure I'm not the first mook to shout that at him. As he turned around, he recognized me and let me know he was a fan of mine and of *Opie & Anthony*. We chatted briefly, and he expressed interest in coming to a show someday.

The rest of the night was spent trying to fuck a girl I had a crush on when I lived out there. She wouldn't fuck me because she had a boyfriend, but would instead let me put my nose under her arms and smell her pits. I understand that doesn't look good on paper, but we had some sort of odd chemistry and my dick would jump through the roof. Many nights were spent in my car, my nose buried under one of her arms, rubbing my helmet through my jeans. Writing this is reminding me of her, and bringing back the regret of never having fucked her. (I never smelled her feet either. I know now what I'll be jerking off to later.)

Fast-forward a couple of years to May 2008, and I'm hosting the four pilot episodes of *Down and Dirty with Jim Norton* on HBO. Our second night of taping, I got word backstage that Robert Iler had requested tickets. Since I *never* have celebrities attending my shows, I was psyched to say the least. I found out where he was sitting so I could do my celebrity shout-out. You know, just letting the folks see that I'm popular in all circles.

He was sitting stage right, about six rows back in a green hoodie. The hoodie instinctively told me he was trying to fly under the radar, so I respected that by announcing, "Ladies and gentlemen, you know him as A.J. from *The Sopranos* . . . How about a hand for Robert Iler!" Hindsight dictates that I was being a selfish scumbag; he obviously just wanted to blend in and relax, and I had just sentenced him to at least a hundred cell phone pictures. Guys in tank tops with cigarette breath would have their arms around him, quoting *Sopranos* lines while their fat girlfriends fumbled like chimpanzees attempting to operate their camera phones.

As far as I was concerned, that was a "Robert" problem, so I was feeling quite good about myself as I sauntered backstage. Until I casually got word from the stage manager that I had mispronounced Robert's last name. "Huh?" "Yeah," he informed me, "it's pronounced *Iler* (Eye-ler), you said *Illier* (Eel-eeyer.)" My response to the stage manager was, "But . . . but . . . I've always said it like that," as if this would suddenly make everything copacetic. I couldn't have given a more idiotic response

Me with Robert Illier (exactly how I spelled it when I uploaded it to iPhoto the night I met him in Los Angeles).

if I'd stomped my feet, pulled down my jeans, and fired a Mars bar onto his pantleg.

It took a moment to process the fact that I had not only butchered my first celebrity introduction, but I did it with HBO cameras rolling in front of fourteen hundred people. The stage manager then gave me the peachy news I'd have to redo the intro if I wanted HBO to keep it in. Really? You mean they don't want one of the stars of the biggest show in the network's history introduced incorrectly by an almost-middle-aged flop from New Jersey?

As the show ended, I took what felt like a five-mile walk to the microphone to admit my humiliating mistake to the audience. Less shame would have washed over me if I were making a confession in the Jon-Benet Ramsey case. Avoiding eye contact with him in the crowd, I informed them I'd mispronounced Mr. Iler's last name as Illier, and then, in true jerk-off fashion, added that I'd always said his name like that. (For some reason, I felt less retarded stressing the fact that it wasn't only that night; I'd never said his name correctly.) But, of course, I couldn't let it end there. I told them I was going to reintroduce him, this time pronouncing his name properly. So I'd not only introduced him incorrectly, I then went back out and made everyone uncomfortable by shining a spotlight on the error. I then notify everyone that we're going to strap in and do it again, thus completing the Douchebag Trifecta.

I went through the same intro as before, this time not fucking it up. Robert was very cool about it; he nodded and waved politely, undoubtedly fighting the urge to hammer a pipe bomb into my rectum. I didn't get a chance to see him after and apologize, so if he's reading this—sorry about that, man.

As I finish this chapter, I am hoping none of you noticed the absolute pomposity I displayed in assuming that after I publicly shredded his name, Robert's going to run out and buy my book. I'm a boob of an unparalleled magnitude.

FIVE WAYS I COULD HAVE HUMILIATED MYSELF EVEN MORE AT MY OWN HBO TAPING:

1. Instead of mispronouncing his last name, accidentally introducing him as Robert De Niro, Robert Townsend, or Robert Kennedy.

2. After introducing him to the audience, point at him, wink, and say, "Thanks a bunch for coming, Robbie."

3. Doing an uncomfortably long impression of a *Sopranos* scene he was in, to show off what a big fan I am.

4. In an attempt to blend in, put on a heavy goombah accent and introduce him as "my paisan."

5. Announced to Robert that in an effort to make it up to him, I'll dedicate a poorly written chapter in my mediocre book to the incident.

Dr. Phil Is a Cunt

THERE'S JUST something about Dr. Phil that makes me want to attack him with a blowtorch. I'm not sure if it's that irritating, singsongy Oklahoma drawl or the fact he looks like Jeffrey Tambor in *And Justice for All*. America was first exposed to this yokel in the mid to late '90s when he started appearing on Oprah's show. Americans, dumb clucks that they are, fell in love with him. The fact that this arrant putz has become a cult figure in this country is enough to make you root for pestilence and global warming.

Probably because of his voice and comfortable delivery, he comes off as stern but trustworthy. Dr. Phil (or as I like to call him, Mr. Potato Douche) is a very calm, confident speaker. He's the first guy I'd call to help me sell a used car, but when it comes to mental health, I'd rather session with Hannibal Lecter.

Since the first time I saw him, he's come off like a snake oil salesman. Like most gurus who give great advice, then do whatever they want in their abysmal personal lives, this tool writes books called *The Relationship Rescue Workbook* and *Dr. Phil Getting Real: Lessons in Life, Marriage, and Family*, yet I never hear him talking about his first marriage. His first wife claims he was a bit of a controlling dickhead who liked to fuck other women. She also said that when she confronted him about his infidelities, he didn't deny them. Instead, Dr. Phil and his brass balls apparently tell her that the infidelities had nothing to do with his feelings for her, and that she should grow up because that's the way it is in the world. Of course, this almost makes me like Dr. Phil a whole big bunch. Had it worked, had she stayed married to him after he set her straight about deep-dicking other broads, I'd have signed posters of this eggheaded zilch all over my apartment. He'd be my hero. And I'm not judging him because he got married in his early twenties and it didn't work out. Hell, I'm thirty-nine and can't keep a woman in my life longer than one baseball season. Nor do I judge him for cheating, if he did. Who knows what those circumstances were—maybe his ex only enjoyed fucking on special occasions, like full moons and the passing of Haley's Comet. Or maybe Phil liked blow jobs, and she steadfastly refused to juggle his bag no matter how high he lifted his asshole off the couch. Or, keeping it simple, maybe her pussy smelled like a wet Irish setter and he couldn't take it anymore. Whatever the reason, if he fucked other women, I'm all for it. As a matter of fact, I'm so all for it, I venture to say, "You go, Dr. Phil!"

If he did indeed wreck that marriage with a wandering cock, my only issue is that he only seems to mention it in passing, and never with details. So it's hard to think of him as anything but a smooth-talking shit-tum who sounds smart but doesn't live smart. (Hmm, that almost reminds me of a Dr. Phil life lesson. . . .) Or, in all fairness, maybe he does provide details. I have admittedly never read any of his books—perhaps in *The Relationship Rescue Workbook* he has a chapter called "How Not to Ruin a Marriage, Like I Did, by Fucking Anything That Walks." Maybe in this chapter Dr. Flavor Saver Under the Nose points out that when a husband has an erection and his wife refuses to spread 'em because she's finger-rolling her hemorrhoids and watching a *Happy Days* marathon, instead of being unfaithful, the husband should mosey into the bathroom and fervently masturbate into his wife's cold cream. (An alternate solution would obviously be to wait until she falls asleep, then lean over and smell her ass while fucking a pint of room temperature cottage cheese wrapped in a piece of wheat pita.)

Dr. Phil has also become an embarrassingly vocal media whore since his rise to fame began. The first time I noticed it was when naughty Pat O'Brien was doing his mea culpa after the release of his filthy phone messages: "I just wanna . . . stick a carrot up your ass. Then I wanna . . . snort coke off your tits with Barbra Streisand and an aardvark. You are so fuckin' hot. Then I'm gonna paint a smiley face on your clit while two South Africans fuck you in the ass and Betsy laps the cum out of the shag rug with her hands tied behind her back. If you like this, if this sounds fucking hot, when you walk by me . . . wink." (Legal disclaimer!!! I made up some of Pat's quotes to be humorous. His were *much* sexier.) Guided by the wisdom of Dr. Phil, Pat admitted that it was wrong to make those calls. He even went as far as to say he "shouldn't have done that." Powerful, complicated breakthroughs like this are undoubtedly what further put America under the good doctor's spell.

Most recently it was the Britney Spears debacle, when Dr. Blabbermouth visited her in the hospital and then held a press conference. What a jabbering asshole. The great thing about this happening, though, was that the public finally began getting a whiff of Dr. Phil's underbelly. Only a brief summation is required, as everyone alive knows the story: K-Fed sent his bodyguards to Britney's house to pick up their two kids. When they showed up, Britney was hanging from the chandelier by her nipples while her sons ran around the living room holding pans of flaming grits. The bodyguards felt this may be suspect behavior, so they called the police. They were busy wrapping up shooting on an episode of *Cops*, so Dog the Bounty Hunter showed up, fucked Britney's face until she passed out, then snuck the kids out under his mullet. Then an ambulance came and took her to the funny farm. After a team of doctors, all the orderlies, and three valet guys sodomized her, she was released the next morning.

Reportedly, she was packing to leave when Dr. Phil walked into her room and attempted to counsel her. Some thought she was giving him a cold reception when she began screaming things like, "Rape," "Beat it, shitdick," and "Someone call my primary-care physician, Jack Kevorkian." After he hightailed it out of there, he talked to *Entertainment Tonight,* saying, "Britney needs two lobotomies and a Valium drip because she's crazier than a shithouse rat. But how about that piece of ass sister of hers. . . . Who's the lucky dog who fattened that bitch up?" Britney's family was furious, since Dr. Phil had already been told who'd fattened the bitch up (they had it narrowed down to either Marty Feldman, Dennis Rodman, or all three members of Hansen). They also felt he had betrayed patient-doctor confidence when he talked to the media and was later seen at the SkyBar doing the electric slide with Britney's period panties on his head.

But with this newfound scrutiny came some interesting revelations about America's favorite TV proctologist. He had to state publicly that his license to practice had been retired, since it was only good in Texas. This renders the license moot anyway, since Texas psychologists are trained to deal with only three things:

1. Mental trauma due to guilt associated with raping defenseless bovine.

2. Rage issues developed when attempting to purchase a twenty-gallon hat and being informed only ten-gallon hats are in stock.

3. Anxiety disorders related to having black people move within three miles of your home.

So now everyone knew this douchebag was no longer legally allowed to practice, and never had been in California. Watching him try to explain everything away to his mildly retarded studio audience was great. He had that same dopey cadence, and he spoke softly, regally, as if he were Christ trying to gently break it to His disciples that even He occasionally enjoyed freebasing and jerking off to Japanese shit porn. To avoid the issue of being accused of practicing psychology without a license, he stressed that he had gone to visit her as a family friend. He claimed he would have "suggested or recommended the appropriate and trustworthy health-care givers" and that he "made it clear that he of course would not be directly involved in any treatment should that come to pass, because it's well known that he doesn't practice psychology privately anymore." How nice. So, now it's not Dr. Phil to the rescue, it's Dr. Phil the medically impotent asshole referral service. Fuck him.

Of course he had to clarify that he'd opted to do TV and write books to raise awareness about mental health. What a relief. Like a naïve rube, I assumed he did TV and wrote books for the $30 million a year he makes doing those things. You can't deny his amazing success; there have been quite a few TV shows and specials. I can state, with pride, that I've seen none of them and have no idea what they're about. But I'll take an educated guess at the gist of each one.

Dr. Phil: A daily one-hour drama about a psychologist turned charlatan who convinces the shittiest families in America they're just like the Bradys, minus the cocksucking dad and dykey housekeeper.

The Dr. Phil House: (The original house was closed down due to constant neighbor complaints, and this phony had to continue on a soundstage.) A pseudoreality show revolving around the medical equivalent of an Amway salesman and his troubled home life. The outside world knows him as a Superman; this behind-the-scenes look reveals that not only is he not a Superman but that he's not even a Clark Kent. He's more of a JM J. Bullock, with a midget's head and Wyatt Earp's mustache.

Decision House: About a structure in which tough decisions are rendered. Originally titled *Every Fucking House in the Country, Asshole.*

Dr. Can't Practice Shit has also had a number of highly rated specials. Every one of the titles of these exercises in melodrama starts with *A Dr. Phil Prime-Time Special.*

Family First: "Heartwarming. Poignant. Dogshit." This was the review given by *TV Guide*. A show all about the family, and how one should place them first. Unless there are more fun things to do. If this is the case, any place from second through twentieth will do. Anything after twenty-first place could cause family members to begin feeling left out and inspire your children to commit patricide.

Romance Rescue: Based on *Animal Rescue*, this is about finding romance for fat and ugly people. Dr. Phil took a hidden camera crew to a mall in the Midwest and attempted to find lovers for people based on deformities (cleft palate for the cleft palate, cripple for the cripple, phone friend for the burn victim, etc.).

Behind the Headlines: In-depth courageous exposé that uncovers the psychological truths behind celebrity meltdowns. Reveals that Margot Kidder isn't actually a certifiably nutty bitch, but just happened to be picking berries for a pie when she was found nude in a neighbor's yard behind a bush. And Christopher Reeve's accident was revealed to be a fake! Turns out he bet a friend fifty bucks that he could go ten years without moving a muscle. The segment ended with hidden camera footage of Reeve jumping out of his wheelchair and kicking a Jehovah's Witness in the cunt.

Escaping Addiction: Observes the day-to-day activities of an active heroin addict attempting to clean up his life. We see his bottoming out and eventual admission into a treatment program. Dr. Phil counsels him daily via text messaging, which is ineffective since the addict is forty-nine with a kindergarten reading level. After the addict's emergence from the treatment facility, Dr. Phil takes him to Waffle House for his favorite meal of fried pig balls and hash browns, with a side of orange marmalade (Dr. Phil's favorite meal, not the junkie's). For dessert, the drug addict is given coffee with milk and heroin, causing him to relapse and die, giving the show the sought-after slapstick ending.

Love Smart: To analyze the sexual problems experienced by four married couples, Dr. Phil goes undercover as a large dildo. After use, and once he's been put back in the sock drawer, he talks quietly into a handheld video camera as he baby-wipes shit and vaginal juices off of his face.

Escaping Danger: Dr. Phil hooks electrodes to the genitals of his studio audience and zaps them with sixty thousand volts whenever they unwittingly put themselves in danger. Frequent mistakes included having unprotected anal sex with people bleeding from the eyes and speaking Creole, and driving through black neighborhoods with the windows rolled down. For lesser offenses, such as swimming right after eating or firing a rifle at a commercial airliner, Dr. Phil simply administered a quick back-whipping with an electrical cord.

Escaping Addiction 2: A one-hour special that spends the first fifty-eight minutes recapping the first installment. The final two minutes are spent promoting his upcoming prime-time special: an undercover exposé about four cameramen who capture amazing celebrity footage when they spend five days inside Lindsay Lohan's uterus.

Finally, Dr. Phil had to publicly admit he'd handled the Britney situation badly. And while he didn't go so far as to say "I'm a phony, incompetent blight who's done less for the medical community than Josef Mengele," he did allow that he "wasn't helpful to the situation" and admitted that if he had it to do over again, he probably would have just "snuck into her room while she was sleeping and fingered her." A sincere apology that wasn't just done to appease the media would have ended with a manila envelope and an R. Budd Dwyer tribute.

A misstep with the media by getting carried away in the moment would be more forgivable if Dr. How's My Profile had never had any trouble before. But in 1989, sanctions were imposed on him for hiring an old therapy client to work in his office, which is a no-no. As a result, he had to take an ethics class, undergo a psychological evaluation, and scrawl *I will not hire schizophrenics to file my papers* a thousand times on the blackboard with an AIDS needle. The woman in question was nineteen and claimed there was a sexual relationship. Dr. Phil countered that the relationship was purely professional, and that he only masturbated into her sandals while she was out to lunch or hemorrhaging in the bathroom.

Despite all of his previous failures, you really can't blame him for attempting to go into the weight-loss business at one point, considering the combined weight of his studio audience on any given day is the same as a neutron star. He sold shakes, supplements, and energy bars. The Federal Trade Commission promptly launched an investigation, and Dr. Got a Little Greedy yanked his weight-loss crap off the shelves and obviously neglected to then take them himself.

Another aspect of Dr. Phil's empire that makes me want to wretch is how popular some of his simplistic, idiotic little sayings have become. They're known as "Philisms" (yes, you read that right), and simpletons all over the country try to live by them. Since I don't know their origin in Dr. Phil's life, I've had to guess at what he was doing or thinking when he created them.

What in the hell were you thinking?

Question asked by police officers when they arrested Dr. Phil for setting his penis on fire to protest deforestation.

I Hate Your Guts

I've been doing this for more than thirty years.

Dr. Phil's angry retort when being instructed as to how he could better deceive his audience.

Are you nuts?

The question Dr. Phil asked of the two fleshy orbs resting on his chin as he was being face-fucked.

You choose the behavior, you choose the consequences.

What Dr. Phil neglected to say to himself when he was hiring manic-depressives as office managers, putting diarrhea-inducing energy drinks on the market, or blathering on to the media after bum-rushing a psychotic pop star in the hospital.

This is going to be a changing day in your life.

What I hope some angry black orderly someday says to Dr. Phil while holding up diapers.

I want you to get excited about your life.

The mantra Dr. Phil was overheard screaming in Terri Schiavo's face when she neglected to respond to him.

Children are very perceptive.

An accurate thought to have whenever you hear a child under the age of eight referring to Dr. Phil as an "irritating psychology hack."

If it's happening now, we're gonna deal with it now!

What Robin McGraw yells at Phil when he has once again failed to achieve an erection.

Get a life.

Dr. Phil's favorite thing to say when he wants to sound like a spoiled teenage girl instead of a man in his fifties.

We're going to start putting some verbs in our sentences.

The best thing Dr. Phil ever said to Rich Vos.

This relationship needs a hero.

Advice Dr. Phil gave to a young Adolf and Eva when they came to him for counseling in 1933.

I am your mother!

What I wish Andrea Yates had said to a young Dr. Phil.

People tend to like easy-to-remember catchy phrases or expressions. They're fun to spit out at a party; whatever pig you're attempting to fuck in the guest room will think you're keen and insightful. More times than not, they're based in common sense and show no true insight at all. "The Ten Life Laws of Dr. Phil McGraw" are exactly that—ten things a retard could have come up with (and did). People tend to mistake his simplistic dumbness as tough love being delivered bluntly.

Dr. Phil McGraw's First Life Law: You Either Get It, or You Don't

This is also the philosophy some people have about the chicken pox, cancer, and Dennis Miller's act. And it's total nonsense, because he listed the only two possibilities in every scenario on earth. He could have just as easily named this one "Heads or Tails," "Fifty-Fifty," or "Six of One, Half a Dozen of Another."

Dr. Phil McGraw's Second Life Law:
You Create Your Own Experience

Another simplistic "no shit" statement. You know what else you create? Your own burger at Burger King, fucktard.

Dr. Phil McGraw's Third Life Law:
People Do What Works

Oh yeah? Well some people do what doesn't work. Back to you, Phil.

Dr. Phil McGraw's Fourth Life Law:
You Can't Change What You Don't Acknowledge

Another excellent point, doc! When you're on television, I acknowledge you, then change the channel. Die.

Dr. Phil McGraw's Fifth Life Law:
Life Rewards Action

And the cavalcade of original thoughts continues. This is a dull rip-off of expressions like "Faith moves mountains, but bring a shovel," "Actions speak louder than words," and my personal philosophy, "Push it in up to the knuckle, I'm gonna cum."

Dr. Phil McGraw's Sixth Life Law:
There Is No Reality, Only Perception

I'm surprised to hear such a New Agey philosophy from such a dyed-in-the-wool lump of shit. I am also relieved. Now when I meet Dr. Phil, I can kick him in the balls, he'll perceive himself to be eating ice cream, and we'll both walk away winners.

Dr. Phil McGraw's Seventh Life Law: Life Is Managed, Not Cured

Yet another meaningless sentiment that could just as easily be applied to a terminal disease. How about making this one a little more fun: Life Can't Be Cured . . . but Hams Are! Dr. Phil is a schlemiel.

Dr. Phil McGraw's Eighth Life Law: We Teach People How to Treat Us

I couldn't agree more. How about a couple of examples . . .

1. When my girlfriend has the flu, or isn't feeling sexual due to a death in the family, she is teaching me to go out and fuck her friends.

2. I had unprotected sex with a prostitute, and she taught me how to get a prescription for Valtrex.

3. When you purchase a Dr. Phil book, you are teaching people in Barnes & Noble to treat you like a blithering idiot.

Dr. Phil McGraw's Ninth Life Law: There Is Power in Forgiveness

While there may be power in forgiveness, there is even more power in lobbing a Molotov cocktail through someone's dining room window. Murder for hire tends to have an empowering quality as well. When all is said and done, though, nothing will make you push out your chest further than a good old-fashioned pederast rumor about that special someone.

I Hate Your Guts

Dr. Phil McGraw's Tenth Life Law: You Have to Name It to Claim It

Definitely my favorite of the life laws because it rhymes. Rhyming is so wonderful because it helps me to remember important things! For instance, whenever I leave my apartment or exit my car, I say to myself, *Where are my keys, please?* Or how many times did I masturbate over the sleeping form of a woman and quietly remind myself, *Don't grunt or you'll wake the cunt.* (This is more fun than I originally anticipated.) To avoid getting my girlfriend pregnant, I had to remind myself to employ an alternative method of lovemaking, *Shoot a load in her dumper, or her gut will get plumper.* And this one I say every day even though I never need to be reminded of it, *It would be such a thrill to kill Dr. Phil.* One too many? Fair enough.

One of my favorite parts of researching Dr. Phil (aside from knowing I was going to get to shit all over this dunderhead) was reading posts about him by angry fans. It was hilarious how wounded these people felt . . . how betrayed. They got so mad at Dr. Phil, and some of the cornball names they called him made me howl. Or maybe these aren't funny; maybe I'm just overtired and behaving like a giddy dunce. Either way, here a few that tickled my ribs:

- Stay in California, Dr. Shill! (This same nerd referred to Britney Spears as "Bratney.")
- There's often little difference between a guru and a sc-rew.
- This article is B.S.! Dr. Phool didn't cancel anything. . . .
- Dr. Phil has gotten too big for his britches. I never fell for his method of pop. (I almost decided against including this one due to its harshness.)

- Will someone silence Dr. Flipping Phil?
- He stepped into the white-hot light of Britney's world. It's so hot, it's more like an X-ray, and it exposed what's beneath the surface of Dr. Phil's behavior!
- Britney released with Dr. Phil. This is a case of wacko meeting quacko.

I hope this wasn't too ruthless an ending for the chapter. Accusations of being too big for one's britches may seem unduly vicious. But all is not lost; like all of us there is a road Dr. Phil must now travel to heal the wounds of the past.

SOME "TOUGH MEDICINE" FOR DR. PHIL:

- Your next prime-time special should be an hour-long psychological profile on the horse who fucked the guy to death in Seattle.
- Invite Dr. Laura Schlessinger onto your show to participate in a panel discussion on the benefits of clitoral circumcision.
- Buy a large pair of britches, so you'll grow into them.
- Become an outspoken segregationist.
- Make a hidden camera sex video of yourself fucking Dr. Joyce Brothers in the rump. As you pound away, be passive-aggressive and backhand compliment her appearances on *Hollywood Squares* and *Match Game*.
- Whenever the subject of homosexuality comes up, just wink and say, "If it smells like fish, a tasty dish—if it smells like cologne, leave it alone."

A Certain Scumbag Security Guard

There's a fat Dumpster-breath security guard here in New York City who I pray is being diagnosed with liver cancer as I type this. It was the night of an *Opie & Anthony* event, and we had a sold-out house of about eighteen hundred people. Being a part of the show, I had an All Access pass and was trying to get my friend backstage. He stopped her, and aggressively, so I told him she was with me. He starts in with this snotty "I don't even know who you are" shit. Unfortunately, I'm not Chuck Zito, Rampage Jackson, or Jim Norton with a gun. The joy I'd have gotten out of giving him the old "Sirhan Sirhan" is almost indescribable.

The worst part about him, including his moist otterish face and obesity, was his breath. Honest to God, it smelled like someone dumped that awful liquid that leaks out of a garbage truck onto a severed cow's tongue and glued it to the back of his throat. I couldn't comprehend how anyone with such a slaughterhouse odor wafting out of his mouth could do anything but whisper. No matter how angry I was, if my yapper smelled like that, I'd only talk through clenched teeth out of the side of my mouth.

So I explained to this douchebag that I'd give my pass to my friend, which prompts him to threaten me with expulsion from the venue. Finally, my agent came down to get me, because an HBO exec had come down to see the show, and I didn't need him to see me slugging an endangered species in the face. (And more important, I didn't need him to see the endangered species slugging me back and knocking me unconscious.)

You've all dealt with cockroaches like this: power-hungry fucking nobodies. These people are meaningless, emasculated zeros in their personal lives who feel the need to try to wield some sort of dignity-saving sword around the rest of us. Picture every scummy I'm-not-a-real-cop traffic cop you've ever dealt with, put horse manure in their mouths, mash them together, and you have this asshat.

I know these guys have a job to do and they deal with assholes all night, but this guy was obviously just born a jerk-off. He probably can't help it—this is just what God meant him to be. I've worked in many venues all around the country, and I've never had an altercation of any kind with security. Ever. As a matter of fact, at the Security Guard National Awards Dinner, I was given the award for Boy Most Likely to Brighten a Security Officer's Day.

I'd love to tell you the night ended with me karate kicking a hoagie down his fat throat and choking him to death. Or even something less dramatic, like running a raised forklift into his stomach or piping mustard gas into the bathroom while he was on the bowl taking a White Castle shit. But those would be falsehoods, mere masturbatory fantasies. In reality, I didn't see him again. I stayed upstairs and fumed, then forgot about it. My lovely friend and I (she finally got backstage) had a pleasant chitchat about the negative effects Dramamine has on my erections, then traded a few lighthearted brown shower anecdotes. She decided to call it a night, because she was getting up bright and early the next morning to have a third-trimester abortion.

Shortly after she left, I remembered that not only had she and I never had sex but that we'd never even fooled around. Nothing had ever happened between us. And I mean *nothing*: no kiss, no hug that lasted a bit too long, not even the accidental rimjob a friend will sometimes give while standing behind you on a ladder. Nothing. She'd never even indicated any attraction to me outside of friendship. She really was just a pal. And I almost came to fisticuffs with Wilfred Brimley's retarded brother over her. I can't decide if that makes me a sincere, consistent guy or a pathetic cuckold. Actually, I can decide. It's fairly obvious, don't you think?

HELPFUL HINTS FROM JIMMY

Although my relationship with this manatee is irreparable, there are things he could do to improve his own meaningless life. Let's start with his **breath**. What he probably needs to do is change his morning ritual by brushing his teeth instead of drinking sardine oil and blowing the dog. Then, perhaps instead of chewing tobacco and swallowing the spit, he could take a stab at flossing.

Clearly, there is also the issue of that gelatinous mass he calls a **body**. A little exercise can go a long way. (I have it on good authority that his sit-ups phobia began many years ago when he threw out his back trying to suck his own cock on prom night.)

Finally, he may want to reconsider that ridiculous Magnum, P.I. **mustache**. Unless they're being used to cover a harelip the size of a geoduck clam, mustaches are fucking *terrible*. And they look equally terrible on everybody. If Tom Selleck couldn't pull off the fat mustache (and he couldn't), what made this woolly mammoth think he'd be the exception to the rule?

So there you have it. Just a few simple steps, sir:

1. Hose out that festering gout wound you call a mouth.

2. Every morning, do five sets of 300,000 sit-ups.

3. Shave that unkempt half-a-cunt under your nose.

4. Assert your power and masculinity by yelling belligerently as you struggle to fit the entire barrel of a shotgun in your mouth.

5. Pull trigger. If desired effect is not achieved, yell, fit, repeat. Blowing your head off won't improve your quality of life at all, but knowing you've done it sure will improve mine.

People I Wanted to Kill on Sight: Part Two

- The guy in the elevator in my building last week who didn't say hello back after I said it to him. What an aloof douche. We've never spoken, although we see each other in the gym a few times a week. I tried to be friendly with a "Have a good one," as I was exiting, and he stared at me like I was doing the Watusi in a shithat.

- Bob Kelly, for blathering on about his new video camera as I try to write. We're at the Comedy Cellar, and he's showing me footage of two Puerto Ricans that he took that afternoon: "Duuude, look at the zoom. The zoom on this thing is friggin' sick!" He then zoomed all the way in for a close-up of them sipping their beverages. If I were half a man, I'd drill my fist into that camera lens and drive the viewfinder back into his fucking eye socket. He just handed it to me in an attempt to woo me with how light it is. A pinless grenade would be less tempting to throw.

- The piece of shit parking attendant who worked in the parking garage in my old building. Not one courteous word in two years out of this broken-English-speaking cock-sucker, and whenever I drove into the garage, he'd always open the door high enough to drive under, but too low for my antennae to clear. I'd hear that vibrating *thwang* sound as it hit the garage door above me, and want to floor the gas pedal and crush him against a wall. Hopefully he moved back to whatever Third World cesspool he was from and found himself being burned alive in a military coup.

- The table of ugly *cunts* at the Comedy Cellar the other night. The fat one kept talking in between shoveling hummus into her face while I was onstage. I told her to shut up. When she refused to stop talking, I threatened to put my dick print in her hummus. The crowd laughed. Then her ugly bird-faced fucking friend threw a piece of pita at me.

Asshole Keith Olbermann

IF THERE'S one thing I hate, it's someone pretending to be what he's not, whether it's Clay Aiken holding hands with a girl, or Larry King pretending to still be alive. But I especially hate when that someone tries to come off night after night as an "in your face" pundit, when deep down he's nothing more than a company man who does nothing more than toe the company line. And that's all Keith Olbermann is. I am completely fed up with his horseshit rage, his desperately trying to be seen as the nemesis of Rush Limbaugh and Bill O'Reilly. He's trying too hard to be the guy who "stands up to the bully": "Boy, did you hear Olbermann last night? That fella doesn't take any guff . . . he's not scared of anybody!" That kind of shit. I felt it would be fun for the whole family if I expounded on my disdain for him. In an attempt to keep it substantive, I'm leaving out obvious atrocities like those purposefully nerdy glasses and bad-wig hairdo.

Reason #1

My complete loathing of this transparent jackoff started during the Imus controversy. Imus's firing was such a galvanizing event because it gave people a chance to talk about race safely. It gave them a chance to feel empowered, like they were doing something to right a long history of wrongs. But it was pandering and fraudulent. A bunch of knee-jerk reac-

The great thing about Olbermann is that even on his nights off, you can still enjoy his hair in *Hawaii 5-0*. Douche.

tionary liberal idiots once again paternalistically patting black people on the head, trying to show that *they* were the good white people, the ones who weren't racist. Hall monitor faggots like Olbermann came crawling out of the woodwork, each one of them wallowing in emotionalism. All of them taking every opportunity to call Imus a racist simply because he made racist jokes. There is a difference, and these talking-head scumbag pundits knew it.

I'll never forget that bison-headed pussy-boy sitting with Jesse Jackson (kneeling there with his mouth open would be more accurate) and groveling, *begging* for approval, after MSNBC announced it was canceling Imus's show. Olbermann is supposed to be this brash tell-it-like-it-is pit bull, yet this is what he had to say: "I was one of those NBC employees who put it out to my bosses behind the scenes that this could not stand, that this change involving Don Imus had to be made. I can say that now, I respected my employers and did not say it until they reached this conclusion, which I applaud sincerely."

This is all you need to hear to know *exactly* who Keith Olbermann is. This fucking turd ran around behind the scenes whispering to his bosses that they should dump Imus. Can you honestly think of anything you hate more than some drip who runs around behind the scenes to the bosses? I can picture him poking that Mount Rushmore skull into every open office door and asking for updates, and then reiterating his boring points about what was appropriate and what wasn't.

Yet he "respected his employers" too much to say it publicly until they made a decision? Jesus Christ, you're a fucking sham. Sounds to me like you were playing it safe there, pit bull. Sounds to me like you weren't willing to stick your dick out in the wind, because if MSNBC decided to stick with Imus (as they should have), you'd look like the politically correct hall monitor cunt that you really are.

And the other side of it, of course, is that Mr. In Your Face was afraid of upsetting his bosses. Why not yell and scream for them to fire Imus publicly, and just take the chance that they won't and you'll have disagreed with them on air? You appeasing, apple-polishing jizzbucket. Opie and Anthony and I are CBS employees, yet we didn't wait for the bosses to "make their decision" before we made our opinions known. We repeated ourselves ad nauseam defending Imus. When CBS fired him, we disagreed publicly and loudly, as did guys like Mike Francesa and Chris Russo. And as a credit to Les Moonves and the rest of the CBS, not once did they ask us to curb our opinions or change what we were saying in any way, shape, or form. We disagreed and the company was fine with our disagreeing (or more accurately, they didn't give a shit about our disagreeing; Imus got the boot anyway). But not Keith, no sir. Keith had to look both ways and make sure the coast was clear. Then, and only then, did this ferocious attack dog start barking. (Or maybe it was simpler: maybe he just wanted to be the big name on the network marquee, and that couldn't happen until the bigger, more talented name was gone.)

But his Jesse Jackson bootlicking didn't end there. Olbermann continued: "Let me ask you again about the other people. Is someone like Rush Limbaugh . . . how have they kept their time slots? Will there be an increased effort to either get them to contain themselves within the rounds of decency? Are they on the ropes, are they on probation?" Here Jesse interrupted and attempted to form sentences, which were allegedly in English. Olbermann strikes me as one of those white elitist scumbags who, deep down, is terrified of blacks. Guys like him are not only afraid of black people but they're also afraid the intellectual superiority they feel over blacks will be obvious. So, what do they do? They pander and over-compensate. Do you see what he's doing? Do you see how this pansy wants a guy like Limbaugh, who is far more respected and quoted than he is, to be silenced? How has Rush kept his time slot? Umm, ratings, you lunk-headed pussy. Ratings. This is exactly what the desperate-for-approval teacher's pet says to the teacher once he has the teacher's ear. He starts snitching on everyone, trying to get them in trouble. After hearing this I had zero, and I mean zero, respect for Olbermann. Why are liberals always so anxious to have other people penalized for saying unpopular, or even shitty, things? You know which two guys came out and said they'd go back on Imus's show after he apologized? John McCain and Rudy Giuliani, two conservatives. Figures.

Reason #2

If the Imus controversy wasn't enough to make you hate this socialist windbag, then the way he sold David Schuster down the river should. Schuster is an Emmy Award–winning journalist for NBC News and MSNBC. Personally, I have no feelings for him one way or the other. I have no desire to see him fired, nor would I lose a minute's sleep if he were attacked in South Central Los Angeles and raped with a cheerleading baton.

During a debate on *Tucker* (a typical political borefest of a show, since canceled), Chelsea Clinton's role in her mother's increasingly pathetic campaign came up. A panel of learned, fascinating men were debating the appropriateness of her role, when Schuster remarked, "Doesn't it seem like Chelsea's sort of being pimped out, in some weird sort of way?" The dullard he was talking to went on to say she wasn't, and then blah blah blah. I tuned out because he was, as I've implied, a lifeless mannequin.

Well, as you can expect from this dick-tucked-back-between-the-legs society we live in, there was "outrage over his remark"! It seems as though the only thing Americans love more than baseball and apple pie is outrage over unimportant remarks. Hillary couldn't wait to play the victim and started whining as soon as a microphone was jammed in front of her face, "You know, I am a mom first and a candidate second." (Allow me to jump in here and point out the obvious: she's an irritating self-centered bitch first, a mom second, and a candidate third.) "And I found the remarks incredibly offensive. You know, I can take whatever comes my way, that's part of what I signed up for as a candidate, as an officeholder. But I think there's been a troubling pattern of comments and behavior that has to be held accountable. So, I have sent a letter to the head of NBC expressing the deep offense that I took, and pointing out what has been a troubling pattern of demeaning treatment. And I would expect appropriate action to be taken."

You can almost give stupid Hillary a pass because it involves her daughter, but I'd love to know what troubling pattern of comments and behavior she's talking about. Especially the behavior part. Were MSNBC commentators holding up pictures of Hillary with the mouth cut out and inserting their penises? Or were they going on air wearing pantsuits with foam-stuffed legs and asking, "Who am I? Come on . . . guess." She was obviously using this as an opportunity to put the network in ass-kiss mode in order to get more favorable coverage.

Predictably, David Schuster popped up the next night to offer an apology for his "inappropriate" terminology, then proceeded to apologize to Bill, Hillary, Chelsea, the Clinton pets, Monica Lewinsky, Linda Tripp, the blue dress, the cigar, and any other living or nonliving entity who may have been offended. He was suspended for two weeks anyway.

We now come full circle, back to Keith Olbermann. The night after it happened, this total fucking asshole goes on to *further* apologize, this time on behalf of the network. As much as I hate him and as little respect as I have for him as a man, I was slightly embarrassed for him.

> *By now you have probably heard that on this network yesterday, my colleague David Schuster discussing Chelsea Clinton's role, a first for her, in her mother's campaign, ask a guest, quote, "Doesn't it feel like Chelsea's being pimped out in some weird sort of a way?" I have the greatest possible respect for David Schuster's work. His reporting for this show and others is assiduous, and excellent, and his political insight is keen. All that being noted* (Olbermann's way of saying, "now that the formalities are out of the way, I can be the company man and opportunist prick you've become accustomed to"), *it was still an utterly inappropriate and indefensible thing to say. The Clintons have every right to be furious, hurt, and appalled; many of us here have similar reactions, ones that transcend political parties and politics itself. David has been suspended; it only remains for me to apologize without limit to President Clinton, to Senator Clinton, and to Ms. Clinton on behalf of MSNBC. We are literally dreadfully sorry.*

The first, and most glaring, irritation is how comfortably he used the word "assiduous." Being of moderate intelligence, I had to look it up. One of the definitions was "constant in application or effort; working diligently at a task; persevering; industrious; attentive." Back in grammar school, when I was little more than a rape victim, I remember it was stressed that there were two ways to become comfortable with a fancy new word. The first was to loudly repeat the definition over and over while having your face slapped. The second, and more preferable, was to use it in a sentence. Let's give option two the old college try, shall we?

- (Adverb) When his bosses' balls or assholes are dirty, Keith will drop to his knees and **assiduously** swab the unclean areas with his tongue.
- (Adjective) Keith Olbermann has been **assiduous** in his willingness to throw other on-air talent under the bus in order to appear more compassionate and meaningful himself.
- (Noun) When it comes to being a duplicitous, backstabbing worm, Olbermann's **assiduousness** is awe-inspiring.

I feel better now, that was fun. But back to the matter at hand: shithead's wordy and unnecessary apology. I love the part right after he mentions the Clintons having the right to be "furious, hurt, and appalled" (the way many Americans felt when their president stuck a cigar into the pussy of a fat intern or the way many veterans of foreign wars felt when Hillary lied about being caught under sniper fire in Bosnia), how he has to throw in, "many of us here have similar reactions." Huh? Did you really, Keith? Did everyone at MSNBC really walk around emotionally wounded and tearing up? Is the psyche of the average employee there that fragile when it comes to the Clintons? Or, are you just being a pontificating, preachy bore as usual? And to apologize without limit: gee, that's big of you (not to mention showboaty and utterly meaningless).

And "we are literally dreadfully sorry"? Come on, you fucking drama queen: take your balls out of your purse and stop lactating, for fucks' sake. It's not like Schuster called Chelsea a cunt (in which case a two-week suspension would have been merited). Sure, he could have used a better term, but *dreadfully* sorry? You melodramatic putz. You're trying just a little too hard to have "a moment" there, Keithy. You probably rehearsed that one in the mirror, then stopped to daydream about Bill putting his arm around you some day: *You know, that apology was really eloquent. Thanks for defending my daughter.* Then you'd look him in the eyes, *Think nothing of it, Mr. President . . . it's my job*, and you two would mosey up to the bar and toast each other with cognacs. Or maybe you didn't have that fantasy, maybe that's just an offshoot of one of my fantasies, and in a moment of hatred I'm attributing it to you. Regardless, I find it disheartening that the employees of a major news station were apparently grieving a verbal misstep like it was the Kennedy assassination. Either you're an exaggerating, lying fuck, or someone needs to grind up St. John's Wort in the watercoolers at MSNBC.

Groveling tone aside, what makes me want to cave his head in over this apology is the complete hypocrisy he's displaying. When Schuster said, "Chelsea's being pimped out," no one in their right mind thought he meant literally forcing her to fuck for money. The word "pimping" has become common use in our culture, and people intuitively understand that it's not being used in a literal sense. MTV has a show called *Pimp My Ride*, does anyone really think that cars are being punched in the grille and forced to take cocks into their gas tanks? I know it, you know it, and asshole Olbermann knows it. How do I know he knows it? Because in September 2007, during a rant against President Bush, he said, ". . . And in *pimping* General David Petraeus, Sir, in violation of everything this country has been assiduously and vigilantly against for two hundred and twenty years . . ." and he went on. First and foremost, there's our old friend "assiduously" again. He sure loves that one, doesn't he?

And the reason I italicized *pimping* is because he stressed it, almost spit it out, when he said it. He's talking about the President of the United States apparently making one of his generals take loads in the mouth and bring him the cash. Or, is Keith just using *pimping* to mean, "used inappropriately," as so many of us understand it to mean in that context? I guess this cunt forgot to mention it during his Schuster apology.

Reason #3

Olbermann was asked something along the lines of, "Will the Imus situation have a Janet Jackson effect on radio?" Of course this fucking blowhard took the bait, and went on to point out that *Rush Limbaugh* and *Opie & Anthony* (the only time these two shows have ever been mentioned in the same sentence) won't be able to get away with certain things without being protested. He then mentions that these protest groups "might not be a bad thing." And then, in the style of a true asshole, he goes on to talk about how he knows how to walk the line successfully:

> *I think my career would be testimony to the fact that you can make fun of people without resorting to racial slurs and sexual slurs and the rest of that. I mean, there are lots of options available to you if you want to bust somebody's chops, there are lots of ways to do it that could be mean, and edgy, and still funny, and yet stay within a certain boundary, and uh, I think we've all been lax about this.*

No, your career would be testimony to the fact that even a loud, no talent, bleeding-heart egomaniac with a giant cranium can be successful. And I love how he sets the parameters as to what's appropriate. It's okay to make fun of people, just not about race or gender, huh? How about shoe size, is that okay? Or facial tumors weighing more than ten pounds—

can we touch on those, or is that a bit much? And the fact that he says "bust somebody's chops" like some witless low-level office manager proves he should zip his lip when it comes to humor. What kind of arrogant idiot tries to dictate what the appropriate line is for anyone other than himself? And then douceface goes on to say there are ways to be mean and edgy, yet stay within certain boundaries. Being mean and edgy normally implies that you've stepped over certain boundaries, retard.

The more I write, and the more tedious audio I listen to, the more I hate this self-appointed morality-judging shit stain. He's everything I hate about the left: pompous, boring, and elitist. He desperately tries to portray an image of a shake-things-up rebel, when deep down he's nothing more than the tattletale hall monitor we all hated growing up. I hope while vacationing in Amish country he's raped by a Clydesdale.

KEITH, YOU WILL REMAIN A CUNT
UNTIL YOU AGREE TO:

- Commit hara-kiri with a butter knife and a dildo.
- Hang out in Bedford-Stuyvesant on a Friday night and allow gangbangers to show their appreciation for your parental generosity by breaking a tire iron over your head.
- Go on *Letterman* and read the Top 10 Automobiles Outweighed By My Head.
- Admit that Bill O'Reilly's reputation for having a large cock is what really fuels your feud with him.
- Show how diverse your personal life is by naming at least sixty black friends (in order of genital girth).
- Admit, for the record, the largest object you've ever inserted into your own ass.

The i-Sound-Like-Shit Phone

WHEN THE iPhone was announced in 2007, I had very little interest in running out and buying one. I saw Steve Jobs's demonstration, where he was standing in front of a stupid dark curtain, wearing that shitty black mock turtleneck. He was trying to appear futuristic and mysterious, but it was like watching Mummenschanz. I hated the way he was holding the small silver-and-black rectangle in his hand like it was a tablet containing five of the Ten Commandments. I also detested the way his dainty fingers were lithely and delicately dancing across the glass surface of this scientific marvel; his thin fingers ice-skating like two *Rent* cast members in Rockefeller Center. There was something very self-congratulating about it. And I especially loathed when the iPhone was first announced—that initial demonstration on the giant screen in front of a live audience. As each new feature was demonstrated, these stupid zombies were ooohing and aaahing in amazement like they were watching a cow deal a three-card monte game.

No, I had no desire for the iPhone. I had my Verizon Blackberry, which had amazing reception and a speakerphone that most black guys would be proud to have as the sound system in their Escalades. I couldn't believe the assholes all over the country standing on line for this phone, as if Apple were only releasing six units to the general public. If you actually camp out overnight to buy a phone, chances are once you get it, there's no one you can call who wants to hear from you.

Anthony (of *Opie & Anthony*, of course) and Nathaniel, one of our former producers, both ran out like a couple of Steve Jobs fanboys and bought them. I was surprised those two stupid fruits didn't show up for work wearing his-and-her matching black turtlenecks. I never realized it was possible to want to smash two cell phones that badly. Watching them make calls or peachily text each other made me want to projectile vomit. There is an odd tapping motion someone makes when using an iPhone, due to the glass surface, so they looked like two smiling chimps a-peck-peck-pecking away.

Naturally, it was no surprise when Bob Kelly and his emotional void bumbled into the Comedy Cellar with his brand-new piece of self-examination-avoiding technology. You should have seen this idiot yanking out his iPhone, offering to Google Map any landmark in the country that anyone mentioned, regardless of how casually. He would prattle on about the features of the omnipotent phone ad nauseam, stopping only when someone feigned a stroke or simply dozed off on their feet.

Week after week he'd babble about this goddamn thing, and then one day it happened; I *had* to have one. I don't know what came over me, but some dumb feature he was overusing grabbed me by the spiritual balls and I literally walked out of the Cellar, got into my car, and drove up to the twenty-four-hour Apple store on Fifth Avenue in Manhattan. Weeks of indifference, and suddenly I was, for no explicable reason, a junkie on a mission. Imagine my horror when I walked up to the front door and saw the sign SORRY, WE'RE TEMPORARILY OUT OF IPHONES. "What the fuck do you mean, you're temporarily out of iPhones??" (I actually said this out loud, like an asshole, to the sign.) A wave of nausea washed over me as my mind's eye saw of all the world's injustice—famine, rape, beheadings, and, of course, the greatest injustice of all—me, at four a.m., being stopped in my tracks by this fucking sign. I muttered like a crazy person all the way back to the car, then drove home and consoled myself with a savage, rage-driven masturbatory session.

I drove back there on at least three different occasions and was greeted by that cocksucking sign. It got to a point where I figured they must have gotten a new shipment of phones and just left the sign up on a lark. I finally got my hands on one (thanks to Bob calling the Apple store and asking them to hold one for a "celebrity" friend of his. Imagine their disgust when I moped in and flashed my best "central Jersey celebrity smile"). I got the eight-gig model, a fancy case, some transparent glass covers to protect the surface, and river-danced all the way home.

One amazing thing about Apple products is their ability to "plug and play." Windows sucks a dick because everything is a nightmare to hook up. All I had to do was connect the phone to my computer, and it did everything through iTunes, including telling my old cell phone providers to go fuck themselves. And holy shit did that turn out to be a mistake.

Here's a brief overview thus far of my experience with the iPhone:

✓ APPEARANCE—A+

Extremely thin and sleek, the entire front is glass. You can't deny this is a bad ass–looking piece of technology. I even like the little HOME button in the middle. It would be a winner if it were sold as a display piece for the mantel instead of as a usable phone. (Or, if there was some way to fuck it.)

✓ AT&T, SERVICE PROVIDER—Fat Fucking F

I live on the West Side of Manhattan, which is considered Beirut by AT&T. Cell service in my apartment *blows*: "Hello," "Are you there?" "Can you hear me?" "If you're there, call me back on my home phone," "I can't hear you . . . who is this?" There. That's *every* goddamn conversation I've had on the iPhone in my apartment. I can't tell you how many calls have been dropped thanks to this dogshit service provider. I think Apple would have been better off if they just attached everyone's iPhones with tin cans and Silly String. Or perhaps every phone should come with an orange construction cone you can pick up and shout into. Something. Because AT&T is horrendous. You can't imagine what an asshole you feel like holding a flat piece of glass against your face with no sound coming out of it.

Notice the NO SERVICE message in the upper left-hand corner at 8:00 a.m. Granted, I was in an out-of-the-way, obscure location: Fifty-seventh Street and Sixth Avenue in an office building with giant windows.

✓ SOUND—D

On the rare occasions I am able to hold a conversation on my iPhone that lasts more than twenty seconds, my problem becomes hearing the person on the other end. I tend to drive and talk on the phone (which is illegal in New York City, but I won't tell if you don't! LOL LOL), so I like a good speakerphone. For the iPhone speakerphone feature to be effective, you need to be in a soundproof room with it held up to your ear like a seashell. I cannot fathom how this volume range was okayed in the final product. Who tests the auditory quality of these phones, fruit bats? I have relatively good hearing, unless I'm using my iPhone, which makes me feel like Blair's cousin Jerri from *The Facts of Life*. Improve the speaker-phone option, you pillow biters.

✓ CAMERA—B

You push an icon on the home screen and the camera just opens up. It's a one-button push and shoot, very easy to use. Also good quality compared to other camera phones. Except for the fact that there's no flash. I'd love to walk into the Apple home offices in Cupertino with my dick out and calmly ask, "Why is there no fucking flash for the camera on this fucking phone?" I need the flash, since most of my photos aren't taken in the Mohave Desert at high noon.

As a rule, the camera option is yet another reason I'd like to hunt down random cell phone manufacturers and administer beatings that would fit nicely in *The Passion of the Christ*. They are still putting two- and three-megapixel cameras in phones, when you know these scumbags have the capacity to put in much higher quality ones. Digital cameras have up to twelve megapixels, but the average cell phone takes a picture that would be clearer if it were done by a sketch artist.

✓ VIDEO—F

I would give the video a higher grade, but there is no video. Cocksuckers. Just had to save something for the third or fourth generation release, didn't you?

Two minutes later, maybe now I can make my phone call! Oops, guess not, there goes that pesky NO SERVICE message again. Perhaps I can just yell out the fourteenth-floor window at this point. And, no shit, my home screen picture is predictable.

✓ TEXT MESSAGING—Started as a D, Became an A

I originally despised the idea of having to look down as I text (looking down is necessary, as it's impossible to text by feel on a glass surface). This made texting while operating a motor vehicle virtually impossible. The first week I had this stupid phone, I was driving worse than Jayne Mansfield with Harry Chapin's dick in her mouth.

I finally figured out the "predictive text" feature, which kind of figures out words for you and corrects common mistakes. For example: I recently texted my transsexual friend, "Hey, come on over. And wear that sexy dress I like." My predictive text corrected me, instead sending the message "Don't come over—you were born with a penis, which makes you a man, dress notwithstanding."

This time service just quit in the middle of a texting session. A little easier to understand in this situation, as I was way out in my isolated apartment on Manhattan's West Side. And the text you're reading couldn't be more misleading. Looks like your pal is about to get his dick wet, doesn't it? No such luck. Rachel is the girl who did research for me, and was bringing over a late-night batch of Dr. Phil articles. The only thing more irritating to read than a NO SERVICE message is anything written about Dr. Phil.

✓ MMS (Picture Messaging)—Started as an F, Remains a Fucking F

Remember the camera feature I raved about earlier? Well, if you'd like to show that snazzy photo to a friend, you'd better be sitting on his goddamn lap. The asshole fuck designers neglected to add the ability to text pictures to someone. It's supposed to be the hottest piece of technology in years, yet I can't even use it to send my cock photos to a minor. Nor can I receive photos on it.

To illustrate my point, I took the liberty of sending a photo of my hairless, molestable buttocks to myself from my Verizon Blackberry. When a picture is sent to my iPhone, I get a message informing me that a multimedia message has been sent. I need to go to a fucking computer (since the iPhone Internet has a 14k modem speed in most locations), and go to viewmymessage.com. I then have to enter a ten-character message ID number (in this case it was the easy to remember q05fp19bxv), as well as an eight-character-minimum password (prop3punk). All of this is very convenient when you have lube all over your right hand and have to type lefty so you can view a clit photo as you're jerking off. The photo then appears (if you don't get the typical error message, of course), at approximately the size of a postage stamp. And an even more irritating AT&T service provider fuck-up is that the photos are only available for five days. With Verizon, at least I had an account that the pictures would be sent to, where I could save them to a folder. Not AT&T. As far as they're concerned, once you open the photo, you better save it to your computer, and then enjoy it with the aid of a magnifying glass.

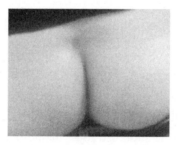

This is the picture, actual size when opened on my computer, of my sniffable keister.

✓ Internal Address Book—C

The address book has potential, but it will remain shit until they install some sort of search feature into it. When you open your contacts, a screen appears with A-Z listed in the right-hand column. You click on a letter, then have to use your finger to scroll down through all the entries starting with that letter. It's fucking annoying, not to mention you look like a homo with your finger swooshing over and over again down the length of the phone. And there's no way to just search, so you always have to scroll through all of your contacts like a boob.

✓ Calendar Feature—A

Very easy to use, one of the more convenient phone calendars I've encountered. Big fucking deal.

✓ Notes Feature—C, Could Easily Be a B+ or an A

The onscreen notepad is very simple to use, and is even yellow like a real live notepad. It looks great and is very convenient. However, what is remarkably inconvenient is that nothing you write on your phone can be downloaded onto your stupid computer. This is a monumental pain in the balls because I jot down a shitload of notes during the day. While writing this masterpiece, I am concurrently working on my third book, *World's Wackiest Hysterectomy Mishaps*. This is to be followed next fall by the launch of my new TV series, *Kids Testify to the Darndest Things*.

Due to events that occurred five minutes ago, allow me to amend an earlier grade:

✓ Internal Address Book—F, You Motherfuckers, F!!

A few minutes ago I was adding a phone number to the contacts section of my iPhone. Something blinked. *And then all of my fucking contacts disappeared.* Every cocksucking one of them. *Gone.* All that remains is my own shitty phone number. If I didn't have most of my numbers synced on my computer, I'd have to go line-by-line through my phone bill to reconnect with certain prostitutes. Something tells me that Mac Geniuses are given that name because they all carry Blackberrys.

So, where does all of this hubbub leave Jim Norton with the iPhone? I have seemingly given the iPhone quite a beating. Reason being that almost every feature on the phone that needs improvement could have been improved before they released it. Almost all Apple products kick the shit out of almost all Windows products (except for viruses, Indian customer service reps, and slow boot times). I don't want the big feature on the second generation of the iPhone to be sending pictures or syncing my nonsensical notes conveniently. I had higher hopes. The second generation of an Apple phone should have wings and a Blu-ray player on it. And you shouldn't require the sonar capability of a sperm whale to fully enjoy the speakerphone. It's unnecessary and aggravating. And insert a goddamn search feature in the address book so I can look for a phone number without making grand, swooping gestures with my fingers. And despite what I've written, and how annoyed I've been at times with this phone, the new one will be out shortly. And the day it comes out, I'm running to the Apple store like a larping faggot to grab mine off the shelf.

iPHONE UPDATE!!

The excitement never stops around here. So, the G3 version of the phone was finally released. *Zzzzzz*, Jesus, what a snorefest. Not one new feature I gave a shit about, so instead of buying it, I treated myself to a rub-and-tug with an Asian woman whose breath smelled like cabbage. You still can't send pictures via text, and of course, no video option. They did add a search feature in the contacts, big fucking whoop.

I downloaded the updates for my version, and loaded a bunch of applications. (Nerds call them applications, hip insiders call them Apps.) I downloaded Scrabble and chess and a subway map and a flashlight and AOL radio and a Rotten Tomatoes application and they all conspired to crash my fucking iTunes. I couldn't sync my phone, and none of the Apps would open. I'm out forty bucks. Fuck the Apps. And fuck the iPhone right in its Home button. But I suppose all is not lost; by 2050 they'll have all the things on the phone they should have put on it to begin with.

Fuck the Yankees

THIS IS probably going to be a tough chapter for me to write, because I've been a Yankees fan since my genitals were tiny and my chest was hairless. (That's right, folks, I was, at one time, an Asian man. THANK YOU VERY MUCH . . . GOOD NIGHT!) Weak, predictable jokes aside, my first sports heroes were all Yankees.

Reggie Jackson was my favorite, despite having the fielding ability of Terri Schiavo. But I loved him anyway. I loved all of them. From that stupid, bowlegged Roy White to blackest-man-in-the-history-of-mankind Mickey Rivers, to Thurman "I'm a Better Catcher Than I Am a Pilot" Munson. They could do no wrong in my eyes. Billy Martin could have taken a watery hangover shit on home plate and I'd still fault the umpire for throwing him out of the game. It didn't even bother me that every pitcher on the staff had a gay porno mustache.

As a matter of fact, I loved the Yankees so much I watched the games in spite of the mindless, incessant babbling of Yankees announcer Phil Rizzuto. Nothing fazed this motherfucker; Chambliss could belt a three-run shot and Scooter wouldn't even break stride on whatever boring trip down memory lane he was in the middle of. I liked Rizzuto, but every time he'd launch into a story about his wife, Cora, I'd want to slam the oven door shut on my head. We get it, Phil, she's a saint on Earth. I'd love to hear more about how her peach cobbler cures testicular cancer, but unfortunately you'll have to shut your face now because Bucky Dent just rapped into another inning-ending double play.

My dad and I went to a few games when I was a kid, but I never spent a lot of time at the stadium. He'd much rather have gone to Shea, as he was a fan of the Transgenders, also known as the Mets. I have always detested the Mets. It began when I was young and one of their games was on, and I had to tolerate Ralph Kiner's shitty accent. (I'm also obsessed with the idea of using Mr. Met to reenact the Robert Kennedy assassination.) 1986 was admittedly tough, because not only did the Yankees completely blow but the Mets played the Red Sox in the World Series. Choosing which one of these teams to root for is tantamount to deciding whether I'd like to drink cum or menstrual blood with my dinner (I recommend the cum if properly aged, but then again I'm a culinary snob).

I did go to a Mets game when I was a kid with a local youth group. My only memory of the day was on the bus headed to the stadium. Me and my childhood friend Bill D'Angelo were sitting together and I cut a slow, lukewarm lactose fart. To date, it's the worst thing that has ever come out of my asshole, including chewed bubble gum and the charm bracelet of a dominatrix. It *eeeaaassed* on out, and slowly, methodically crept to the back of the bus. It was fucking *brutal*. It was sour milk mixed with twelve-year-old boy's leaving his hometown nervousness. Bill wanted to throw up, and as it crept back, passengers were commenting row by row. When some older teenagers from six rows back yelled out, "Jesus . . . who the fuck farted??" I was beet-red with embarrassment. I slumped down in an attempt to remain incognito, and stupid Bill pointed at me and announced, "Him." One of the kids loudly asked what the fuck had died in my ass, and I felt it prudent to mull over my response in silence.

The last baseball game of any kind I attended was Game 2 of the 1995 ALDS between the Yankees and Mariners. The Yankees had won the first game, which was miraculous, because the Mariners had kicked the shit out of them all year. They were the one team I knew the Yanks couldn't beat. Game 2 turned out to be an historic game because it was Don Mattingly's last game at the stadium. He was having a dreadful year due to back problems; I think he finished the season with seven home runs and forty-nine RBIs. It was also a really dramatic game. The Yankees were down by one in the sixth inning. I figured this would be a fine time to get a hot dog. As I'm walking out I hear the crowd roar. I run back just in time to see Rubén Sierra's game-tying home run sail over the fence. What an asshole I am. That's what I get for trying to beat the crowd to the food stand.

Mattingly was up next, but like I said, he was having a shit year. So I resume my plan and walk into the bowels of the stadium to a food stand, and begin watching the game on a monitor. I hear an *eruption* from the crowd, and look up at the monitor to see Mattingly hitting the go-ahead home run. In his first postseason ever, he hits a dramatic shot over the wall in what I know will be his last game at Yankee Stadium, and I'm watching it on television like every other dumb cunt in the country. If I'd had a shotgun, I would have dropped my hot dog down the barrel and blown my brains out with it.

I returned to my seat and the game went into extra innings. It started to drizzle and in the fifteenth inning, Jim Leyritz belted a dramatic two-run, game-winning home run. Truly one of the most exciting moments of my life that didn't have a load spilled at the end of it. (The way things were going, it's a miracle that when he hit it I wasn't in the bathroom testing the erosion rate of urinal mints.) I left the stadium that night very much in love with the Yankees. They went on to Seattle, and the shit stain Mariners swept the next three games and won the division series. Randy Johnson, that lanky, scuzzy fucking giraffe, mowed them down completely. Joe "Itchy Prostate" Torre then joined the team in 1996 and brought four championships in his first five years.

My first negative encounter with a Yankee was around ten years later, in 2005. I was sitting in the Brooklyn Diner on Fifty-seventh Street with Opie and our buddy Tyson Walter, when we looked out the window in time to see a semiretarded face with a Joe Dirt haircut bobbing by, a good four feet above everyone else. Op nods and says, "That's Randy Johnson." He and his perpetually injured back were now pitching for the Yanks (one of many horrendous free agent overpayments made famous by George Steinbrenner). I have always despised him and wasn't about to like him just because he was wearing a Yankees uniform. (My ideal scenario was that the Yankees would win a game that he was knocked out of due to a screaming line drive to the groin.) Of course, because I hate Randy Johnson, I grabbed my camera and dashed out to get a photo with him. Opie, being the consummate trooper, came out with me and agreed to take the shot.

We finally caught up with Lurch at the corner, and I said, "Hey, Randy, I'm a huge fan, could I snap a quick pic with you?" This John Holmes–looking motherfucker says "No thanks" and crosses the street. I can't express how badly I wanted a bus to come zipping through the red light and crash into this ass and his overactive pituitary gland. "*No thanks.*" What kind of response was that? I was asking for a fan photo and he responded like I was trying to sell him a set of encyclopedias.

Let's play a quick game of find and circle the lumbering asshole.

I Hate Your Guts

My eventual hatred of the Yankees began in 2006, with Derek Jeter. He's an odd guy to hate for a lifelong Yankees fan, since he's not only the best shortstop in the history of the team but also one of the most valuable players ever acquired. Actually, it started before that, subtly, in January 2005. Jeter had replaced Cal Ripken as the "face of baseball" in XM's advertising campaign, so he made an appearance at the XM booth at the Consumer Electronics Show in Las Vegas. People were swarming him, so security was fairly tight. Understandable. Because I'm an on-air personality (or lack thereof LOL LOL LMAO LOL), I was brought back into the dressing room and introduced to him.

We shook hands and he agreed to a picture, but somewhere, in the back of my mind, I felt a bit uneasy. Just a quiet thing really, but it was there nonetheless. A small voice in the recess of my mind whispered, *He's a prick*. I didn't even want to admit to myself that I'd heard the little voice. Thinking he was a prick somehow felt like a betrayal. There was just something about the way he looked over my head when he shook my hand. And it wasn't because he was disinterested or even dismissive; I've had plenty of those encounters. That doesn't bother me. Jeter's an icon, I'm a fat-necked, third-mic nobody; so naturally he wouldn't have any vested interest in meeting me. But there was a feeling I got of . . . *dislike*. I felt it when we took the photo, although I can't put my finger on what it was, nor could I then. I sensed he almost looked down on me for asking, like he wanted to say, *You're a guy—why would you be asking me for a picture? What are you going to do with this, just stare at it?* It was that kind of a feeling. I could never prove it in court, but eighteen years of stand-up gives you a kind of sixth sense (and, according to the picture, a second chin, wucka wucka!). But that's neither here nor there; he took the photo without objection, and I spent the rest of my time in Vegas fucking prostitutes.

It's hard to believe these two creatures actually come from the same species. Jeter and I sharing a laugh over what a difference good DNA can make.

Fast-forward a year and a half, and XM Satellite Radio buys a table for $25,000 at Jeter's annual charity dinner. It was a big event, always well attended by players and other celebrities. Eric Logan is nice enough to invite me along with Op and Ant. Of course, the first thing I thought of was getting my photo signed (I've never denied being a self-centered prick). So I throw on my suit, tuck my 8x10s of myself with Jeter and myself with Joe Torre (whom I had virtually assaulted for a photo years earlier in the Vegas airport), and gleefully skip out to the event. The first thing that annoyed me was that the players' dining area had been roped off to everyone else at the dinner. So we couldn't approach them, just stare at them like zoo animals. Now I understand they want to eat without being bothered, but for twenty-five grand a table we should have been able to toss feed at them and sit on their laps during dessert.

I finally got the chance to get the picture signed when I saw Jeter in an adjoining room taking photos with people. I think there was something like a $100 fee to take a shot with him, which was fine because all the money went to charity. So I waited outside the room with my photo in one hand and a Sharpie in the other. Jeter comes out with two security guys, and I present the picture and Sharpie. I am so good at this that I not only have the Sharpie uncapped but it's also pointed toward the photo so all he has to do is grab it and sign. I say, "Hey, Derek, would you mind signing this photo of us together?" I was so specific in my description because people are always presenting athletes with shit to sign so they can hawk it on eBay. I wanted him to know that it was a personal thing that couldn't be sold. He claps me on the back and answers, "I can't right now, buddy, I have to go do an interview. Hit me up later," and keeps walking. I'm disappointed, but I understand, and figure I'll just ask him later. And besides, he called me buddy, and buddies always keep their word!

I'm definitely bummed until Roland (the booker for the *O & A* show) notices that the players are leaving the room to use the same bathroom the public is using. I grab my camera and Roland, and head to the toilets. We hang outside the men's room for a minute and sure enough, here comes Yankee great Ron Guidry. Being a conscientious gentleman, I wait until he is exiting the bathroom before I ask. The last thing I want to do is be turned down for a photo with the Louisiana Lightning because he's turtling. He agrees to the pic, but I get that same stare-over-the-head feeling I got in Vegas. I shake it off, figuring I'm just being a hypersensitive faggot.

Next on the bathroom stalking list is rookie sensation Robinson Cano, who is an out and out fucking asshole. I ask him if we can take a picture (also after leaving the bathroom, not headed toward it), and he answers curtly, "Yeah, make it quick." Hey, fuckhead, I requested a photo, not help with a calculus problem. (I thought this. What actually came out of my mouth was, "Thanks, Robinson," as Roland snapped away.)

Let's see so far: Jeter blew me off, Guidry was completely disinterested, and Cano was an asshole. Great night in the making. Next on the fucko list is catcher Jorge Posada. He wasn't stopping for anyone, and he had a guy with him. The only reason he stopped for me was because I had performed at a benefit his wife had put together. I blabbed this out as he was trying to walk by me and shamed him into stopping. By the disgusted look on his face, you'd think the guy taking the picture was allowing his hard-on to poke through his open zipper.

I look like I'm shitting my pants, and Posada looks like he's being forced to make a hostage video.

Ex–first baseman Tino Martinez walked by and ignored me so completely I momentarily doubted my own existence. Lefty cocksucker. No pic with the Baaam-Tino. When Jason Giambi came by for a tinkle, I figured he'd be the biggest dickhead of them all. He used to play for the Oakland A's and that was enough for me. Well, dip me in shit, I couldn't have been more wronger! He was by far the nicest guy there and took pics with every single fan who asked.

The Giambino looking very natural and relaxed.

Finally, Mr. Wonderful had to release some golden nectar from his holy cock, so I once again took out my photo and Sharpie. Jeter was the only player with two bodyguards around him. Like a five-year-old, I thrust my picture out, asked if he could sign it, and he looked at me and replied, "I can't right now, man," and continued without breaking stride. The moment this happened the little voice in my head found its way to my mouth, and as I turned to Roland I said, "What a cocksucker." Derek had looked at me, made the determination once again that he didn't like me, and neglected to stop. I knew there was something personal about it.

If I were a chick he'd have stopped for me. (Unless I looked the same as I do now, but was female, in which case he'd have said, "Fuck off, you fat dyke," and smashed my clit with his World Series ring.) I really couldn't believe he'd said no, there was no one else in our immediate vicinity. He just didn't fucking want to. I was *livid*. I went back to the XM table miserable and sulking, and ruined everyone else's dinner with my toxic energy.

The one highlight of the evening came when I saw Jim Leyritz, on the Yankees side of the rope, standing close to us civilian pigs. A week earlier, we had Jim in the studio and talked to him for about two hours. He was a great guest, so I figured I could at least mingle with him. I said, "Hey, Jim," and I got a slow nod and a quiet "hey" back from him, then he avoided eye contact.

Ahh, he must be drunk, he doesn't recognize me. Haha, wait until I remind him, he'll feel like the rear end of a horse and then clap me on the back! I said, "I'm not sure if you remember me, we interviewed you in the studio . . ."

"Yeah, I remember you. Hi."

FUCK. What is it about this shitty uniform that turns these guys into such dicks? In hindsight, I realize his being inebriated was certainly possible. I'm very perceptive that way. Once someone is accused of driving under the influence and vehicular homicide, I look back to when they seemed a bit out of it to me, put two and two together, and formulate this boring fucking sentence of filler. I had kind of (*desperately*) hoped he'd lift the rope and introduce me to some of the guys. So I went back to the table with an even worse fun-wrecking energy than I had before.

I Hate Your Guts

Me and Jim Leyritz, right before I bet him ten bucks he couldn't down five hundred shots and still make it home in less than twenty minutes.

As the evening mercifully wore down, I resigned myself to the fact that I wasn't going to get what I wanted. But then I noticed some of the players hanging out on the stage, and fans were approaching them getting things signed! Jeter was onstage, as was Joe Torre, so I marched toward the stage, barreling over people. I made eye contact with Joe, who wasn't signing balls or paraphernalia, and held up my pic. He saw it was the two of us, smiled, and signed it. Now all I had to do was get Derek— he'd sign for me, and all would be forgiven. I made eye contact with him and held up my photo no less than three times. *Three fucking times.* And he looked away all three times. Couldn't be bothered. It was conscious, on purpose, and a total douche move. As he was walking off stage, he motioned for a hot girl to jump onstage, took a photo that this dumb slit will use as her screensaver, and then disappeared behind the curtain. I felt numb. The Yankees captain, this supposed great guy, had just been a complete scumbag to me. I have never, not once, been that much of a jerk-off to a fan (at least not a white one).

The next morning I got some of my frustrations out by smashing his crummy gift bag on the air. That made me feel better temporarily, but when all was said and done, the whole thing bummed me out—a lot. What really bothers me, underneath it all, is that I am a man in his late thirties humiliating himself in front of men who hit a ball with a stick. Things in my career are going well, I have friends, yet around the Yankees, I act like a five-year-old with leukemia. I couldn't have been more pathetic if I had set up a hospital bed outside the men's room and asked every player to "hit a home run for me." Maybe Jeter was right to blow me off. Here he is doing charity work, and I take every dollar I make and donate it to Craigslist. The more I think about it, the more I realize he was correct to hate me on sight. Fuck me.

DO THE YANKEES WANT TO "WIN" ME BACK?

- Let me throw out the first pitch of the season opener, but instead of tossing it to the catcher, let me aim at Mickey Mantle's liver in a jar on home plate.
- Make the entire upper deck of the stadium a Holocaust museum.
- Instead of pine tar, permit me to sticky up Jeter's bat handle with donkey cum.
- Fire longtime Yankee Stadium announcer Bob Sheppard and replace him with a white supremacist.
- On Old Timer's Day, hand every fan fourteen years and older a colostomy bag filled with pudding.

- Force the home plate umpire to announce calied strikes by *Sieg Heil*ing.
- Require any fan who brings a foam hand with the pointed finger to be seated next to someone carrying a foam asshole to jam it in.
- Reheat the rivalry with the Red Sox by sprinkling anthrax in their jockstraps.
- Make the team mascot a monkey who is trained to bite Jeter's balls as he takes warm-up swings in the on deck circle.

The Hat Whisperer

I WAS walking through the school cafeteria one afternoon wearing my normal getup, topped off with a bright-red floppy Kangol (it was the type of hat Henry Fonda would have worn if *On Golden Pond* had been filmed in Compton). Delroy was a junior when I was a senior, and he was fairly well known because he was big and loud. He was the type of black guy white guys are instinctively afraid of, even though I don't think he fought very often. If guys like that ever made shitty remarks to me, I'd always pretend I didn't hear them. Because once you acknowledge you heard it, you're then expected to act on it. And I didn't want to act on it. It was better for people to think I was deaf than a total pussy.

He was at a table with a big group of people, showing off for a bunch of girls and just being a loud cunt in general. Seeing a pasty-white bespectacled douche in a Kangol bopping by must have seemed like a gift from God. I would have been less conspicuous in a yellow sundress. It was obvious they noticed me by the perceptible hush that came over the table. Unfortunately, I was beyond the point of stopping and turning around, so I stupidly forged ahead. That shithead was ogling me as I approached the table, and when I got within striking range he jumped up and *snatched* the hat off my head. I felt his big hand slap the top of my head, and my Kangol, some hair, and what I believed to be scalp leaving my head. Abu

Musab al-Zarqawi employed a gentler touch when removing hats in his home videos.

Because I was so self-conscious about my hair, I reached out and angrily *snatched* it back. This wasn't an act of bravery, by the way. I had the enchanting combination of a greasy bowl haircut with hat head. My awful hair was such a source of humiliation that, in the moment, my instincts decided that a broken jaw would be less embarrassing than walking around for the rest of the day hatless. But since Delroy was young and boisterous, and is probably in prison as I write this, he didn't understand the insecurities of a wigger with cowlicks, so he interpreted my grab back as an act of aggression. He pushed his chest out and yelled, "Oh, you want to fight me? Let's go, motherfucker!" I most certainly did not want to fight him. (In actuality, I wanted to find a seat and spend the rest of my lunch period gathering masturbation fodder by leering at tits and peeking up the skirts of freshman girls.)

Something in his mannerisms told me that he really didn't want to get involved in a fight either; a part of him was mildly surprised that this little weirdo had behaved aggressively. Had I gone outside, I'm sure he would have fought me (or, to be more accurate, savagely beaten me and shit in my hat), but I gave him the face-saving out he needed. By giving him a face-saving out, I mean blurting out what is probably the most wishy-washy, sissyish thing I have ever said. As we were walking outside to the fight/slaughter area, I said, "If you wanted to see my hat, all you had to do was ask." This implied that he wasn't treating me like a total pantywaist by snatching it off my head and laughing but that he genuinely fancied my hat and wanted to take it for a test-drive. It also implied that the tough medicine I was about to administer could have been avoided had he perused *Miss Manners* and learned a little hat-borrowing etiquette.

"All you had to do was ask." Jesus, what a fucking wimp. I could not

have behaved more like a bitch with my shitty hat head and clownishly fat shoelaces. Faced with a potentially violent situation with a 6'3" black guy who has challenged my masculinity, I felt the best course of action was to start talking like my grandmother. I'm surprised I didn't collapse and ask him to put nitroglycerin under my tongue. Thank goodness he didn't steal my social security check and make me fend him off with my purse.

In some lame, desperate attempt to defuse the situation, I said something about not wanting to get suspended. Yet another false implication of manliness: *I'd love nothing more than to engage in fisticuffs, but Mother would throw a fit if I missed that Western civ test.* He took the bait and talked a little shit, but began to walk away.

In hindsight, I wish I had punched his grinning, fucking face with all my might. My injuries would have long since healed, and I'm sure by this time I'd have gotten used to false teeth.

NOW I'M SURE YOU'D LIKE TO KNOW WHAT YOU CAN DO TO BE FORGIVEN:

- Show up at my apartment and gently place a red Kangol on my head. If I pull away shyly, firmly but lovingly hold my head steady and smooth the hat down while asking, "There, there . . . isn't that better now?"
- Pen a thousand-word essay on why one should show empathy for suburban whites with ghetto-envy, instead of exposing them for the sheltered cowards they are.
- Purposefully allow yourself to be infected with Hepatitis A.
- At your next high school reunion, bring up my name as you slice your wrists over the punch bowl.

Eliot Spitzer: Welcome to My World, Shithead

I NEVER liked Eliot Spitzer; there's just something about his face that makes you want to backhand it. His nose and mouth are kind of scrunched up, framed by two freakishly large ears, and topped off with a hairline that belongs on a shift supervisor in Chernobyl. That is, I never liked him until he got busted with a prostitute. Then I kind of connected with him. It made me well up with pride that there was finally a politician who represented my interests. Who would have guessed that I was his constituency?

Every man who's honest with himself understands why Spitzer did what he did. Even if you wouldn't do it, you get it. He gave Ashley Dupree four thousand dollars to fuck her. Women were outraged and disgusted; men wished they had more disposable income. Normally she didn't charge that much, but he had to get her from New York down to D.C. via Amtrak, so there was a minimum number of hours. Ever the fiscally responsible governor, he didn't even put her on the Acela; he stuck her on the local. God, I love him for that—it's so passive-aggressive. *Yeah, I'll pay you four grand, but you're going to stop in Edison, and Woodbridge, and South Philly, and Baltimore. . . .* Being a fellow sex addict, I certainly can relate to the ritual of it. He'd probably check his escort agency ac-

count to see how much he had available, and I'll bet you dollars to dough-
nuts he had a tent in his gubernatorial slacks while he went online to
book her train ticket.

Investigators questioned the hooker and kept trying to get dirt about
Spitzer's sexual proclivities. All she could come up with was that he liked
to fuck with his socks on. The joy that brought me is almost indescribable. It meant one of two things: either he has disgusting yellow talons
and chronic foot odor (which rules) or, more than likely, Eliot was so
lathered up by the time he got to her room, he couldn't even undress
properly. His mouth would be dry as he waltzed into the room with his
cock standing straight up and a clear spot the size of a yarmulke on the
front of his pants. She'd attempt some idiotic small talk as Gollum un-
buckled his belt and did the shimmy-walk over to the bed. He'd lean
forward and literally fall dick-first into her snatch with his pants and
shoes still on. While fucking, he'd kick off his shoes and trousers as he
simultaneously buried his sweaty face in her neck and thrashed around
like a salmon, sans condom. His socks remained on because if he tried to
kick them off, his toenail would scrape his calf.

There's no real mystery as to why he paid top dollar for some early-
twenties pussy. Looking at him and his sexpot of a wife, Silda, during his
humiliating announcement, it was obvious to me that she was a real dullard between the sheets. He's confessing spending a mortgage payment on
a rimjob, and she's staring straight ahead like she has a morphine drip in
her arm. And while she isn't ugly, she looked almost identical to Jeff Con-
away in an ascot. She reminds me of the type of gal who does her nails
while you eat her pussy.

Prostitution scandals enrage women because they intuitively understand they are all vulnerable to the same thing. When men are paying for
sex, we aren't just paying for the privilege of sticking our hogs in the
babymaker. (Although that's certainly a part of it. Nothing worse than

handing over cash to an escort who just wants to be friends.) We are also paying for her *acting*. The more expensive the whore, the better her acting better be. He doled out more than four grand to a sexy twenty-three-year-old because he wanted eye contact, he wanted to be convinced that fucking him for cash is exactly what she had in mind when she ran away from home a few years ago.

My girlfriend and I looked her up online when her picture first surfaced, and of course my girlfriend thought she was ugly. Invariably, she asked what I thought (and the phrasing of her question told me exactly what my answer had better be): "You don't think she's hot, do you?" Ashley was in a bikini, and I had to make a quick scan of the photo to find some sort of flaw. "Nooo, she's ugly. I mean . . . look at her ears . . . they're . . . too close to the top of her head. Who would fuck her over . . . and over . . . and over . . ." My first instinct to shout "Not only is she hot, but I'd eat her ass on top of your dead body" was obviously misguided and better kept to myself. Kind of ironic to insult the looks of a girl who got four thousand dollars to have sex. After the last time my girlfriend and I fucked, I took her to T.G.I Friday's.

ELIOT CAN MAKE EVERYTHING AS RIGHT AS RAIN AND RE-RUN FOR OFFICE IF . . .

- At one point during a debate with Governor David Paterson, Spitzer confrontationally asks, "What the fuck are you looking at?"
- Instead of shaking hands with voters, he lets them smell his fingers.
- During his public apology to Ashley Dupree's family, he insists he had no idea she was twenty-three, but thought she was twelve.

- While testifying at his trial, he holds up a picture of Jim McGreevey and proclaims, "Jesus Christ, at least I wasn't doing what she was."
- He refuses to mention Ashley by name, referring to her only as "the girl with the golden shitter."

That's Right, Asshole—
Still More Book Ideas

- *A Dildo for Milly.* A young woman comes of age after finding a weed whacker in the shed and mistaking it for a masturbation aid. A melancholy tale about the wonderment of self-discovery and chronic guilt, combined with a permanently nicked labia.

- *A Do-Gooder Gone.* Exclusive interviews with the bear who finally mauled Timothy Treadwell to death at the end of *Grizzly Man.* From his own mouth, hear the events that lead up to his being completely fed up with Treadwell and finally deciding to eat him. Will also feature conversations with other bears who were irritated with Treadwell, and even one who is claiming repeated sexual assault. Plus, never before seen photographs of the attack, taken with the bear's own seven-megapixel camera.

- *Look to Your Left, Folks.* A pilot announces to the passengers that if they look out the left side of the aircraft, they'll see the Grand Canyon. Everyone on the plane oohs and aahs, except for Larry-Jean, our transgender hero, who realizes that something is awry: this is a flight from New York to Boston.

- *Undercover in the Mafia.* A crime novel about a Hawaiian detective who attempts to go undercover to break the back of the Sicilian mafia. His cover is blown after two days when he orders a pizza and is seen sneaking slices of pineapple onto it.

- *The Coin.* Teddy Shavers is as ordinary as any of us. He lives alone and leads a quiet, unassuming life as a door-to-door catheter salesman. That is, until he finds "the coin." The pocket of a rented tuxedo turns out to be a looking glass into paradise when Teddy finds a very unearthly nickel, which magically replaces itself whenever he takes it out of the pocket. Teddy fishes into the pocket day and night in an attempt to amass a fortune. He cannot believe this gift he's been given . . . but every gift has a price. With the exception of this one. There is no penalty—only nickels, which culminate in a new sofa eight years later.

Coke and Pepsi
Can Both Suck My Dick

I'M TIRED of being put in the middle of the ugly cola war that's been going on between Coke and Pepsi for the last fifty years. Personally, I prefer Coke—Diet Coke actually. I don't know what kind of crap they put in it, but it's more addicting than Demerol. I'm not a big fan of regular Coke; it's too sugary and sweet and makes me thirstier than when I started. Regular Pepsi is barely drinkable in a pinch, Diet Pepsi is god-awful swill. The only affection I have for Pepsi is that Michael Jackson set his stupid plastic head on fire doing a commercial for it in 1984.

Restaurants, hotels, and other places will only sell one or the other. The Jews and Palestinians share more camaraderie than these cunting beverages. I'd like a Diet Coke, please. Is Diet Pepsi okay? No, bitch, it isn't. I'm aware of the existence of Diet Pepsi—it tastes like piss with St. Joseph Children's Aspirin sprinkled in it. Well, we only offer Pepsi products. Oh, I see. Well I only offer Canadian money, so here's a couple of loonies, asshole. Now go buy yourself a pair of prosthetic tits. See what I mean? You can't just offer people something else when you voluntarily don't carry the requested product. It would be nice if life were this simple: I'd like a blow job, No. Is a yes okay?

These spineless restaurants have allowed the soda companies to pussy-whip them into not offering a choice. It's a minimonopoly. I want to sue somebody for collusion. I don't know who, or if it even is collusion, but it sounds like it could be. I'm just tired of it. You know where they shouldn't carry Coke products? In the Pepsi store. Anywhere else on the planet should have both, you communist shit eaters. Even the goddamn airlines are forced to make this choice. Very comforting to know that as I'm plummeting to my death I won't be able to sip the carbonated beverage of my preference. Can I have a 7UP? We have Sierra Mist. Do you really? That's fascinating. What else do you have that I might be interested in? Gingivitis perhaps? A touch of cervical cancer? These faggot companies can kill each other for all I care, just keep me out of it.

I don't know how we expect gangs and warring countries to make peace when two manufacturers of paint-removing, stomach-rotting beverages can't even share fridge space in a one-star restaurant off Route 80. The only way to stop this war is that we, the public, mustn't stand for it anymore. From now on, whenever I order a Diet Coke and they throw that "We carry Diet Pepsi" malarkey at me, I vow to stand up, pull down my pants, look around the room belligerently, and shit on the floor.

Oh, sure, at first I'll get arrested, it will make the news, and it will probably ruin my career. But if it catches on, if people start shitting on floors all over this nation, then, and only then, will things change. A waitress will mosey over; the customer will request a Coke. And although her establishment doesn't carry Coke, she gives the customer a friendly smile and jots it down. She then bolts out the back door to a convenience store to buy the customer a Coke herself. If history has taught her anything, it's that dashing for a Coke is far easier than cleaning shit out of the cracks in the floor.

Don't be shy about ordering alternative beverages, since another way to force these companies into compliance is to hit them in their pocketbooks. Leading the charge as usual, I've listed a few of my favorite drinks to enjoy with a burger:

WARM PAPAYA JUICE (PULP OPTIONAL)
VISCOUS SHEEP'S MILK IN A BURGER KING
   TUMBLER
SQUID-FLAVORED YOO-HOO
LIVERWURST FIZZ ON THE ROCKS
TUNA CAN WATER
FIVE ALIVE
COLD BLACK COFFEE
CAPTAIN MORGAN WITH A METAMUCIL CHASER
FLOUNDER CUM

South Park
Eyes Jesse Jackson

HERE'S ANOTHER "black leader" who absolutely scares the balls off of white people. No matter what the racial issue may be, and regardless of merit, the instant he and his retarded Billy Dee Williams mustache show up, whitey bends over, grabs his ankles, and thanks the good reverend for the colon-wrecking he's about to get. It's amazing how frightened my fellow blue-eyed devils are to call him out on some of the horseshit he spews. A perfect example was when he began calling himself a Baptist minister in 1968, even though he flunked out of the Chicago Theological Seminary his first year there. If all he had to do is just call himself a minister to be ordained, why didn't this moron drop the reverend nonsense and call himself Dr. Jesse Jackson, OB-GYN. He could then make all of his speeches with his head buried neck deep in a pussy, which would explain why most of what he says comes off as unintelligible, mush-mouthed idiocy.

It's also been said that he lied about being on the balcony with Martin Luther King, Jr. right after James Earl Ray assassinated him. Jackson claimed to cradle Dr. King's head as he lay dying, while others who were there claimed that Jackson was, in fact, in line at KFC waiting for a Boneless Variety Bucket.

What makes him repugnant, though, is the complete drivel he spews about race, considering what a bigoted shitbag he's been. People are undoubtedly tired of hearing about his infamous "Hymietown" quote, especially since it was only reported and isn't something you can watch on YouTube and have a laugh over. While having breakfast with *Washington Post* reporter Milton Coleman in 1984, Jackson was complaining about how certain American Jews are preoccupied with Israel (which is tantamount to complaining about black men being preoccupied with fat white girls or the Irish being preoccupied with Alcoholics Anonymous). He said something along the lines of "All Hymie wants to talk about is Israel; every time you go to Hymietown, that's all they want to talk about." This was fucked-up for a couple of reasons.

First of all, Jews do *not* only want to talk about Israel; they also enjoy discussing diamonds, banking, and controlling the media. Second, although Milton Coleman is black (think fat-faced Louis Gossett, Jr.), he's a reporter. For Jackson to think that he could say something that stupid and inflammatory to a member of the media and have it kept private shows horrendous judgment. Members of the press are even worse secret-keepers than altar boys. Someone should have sat Dr./Reverend/Pope Jackson down and explained to him that reporters are notorious blabbermouths because *it's their fucking job.*

What made matters worse was that once the whole thing started to blow up in his face, he lied about it. And not only did he lie about it, he blamed the Jews for conspiring to defeat him. So let's get this straight: Jesse is black, he bad-mouthed Jews to a black reporter, the black reporter blabbed about it, yet somehow the Jews are persecuting him? Fucking jackass. American Jews were a huge part of the civil rights movement, and I'm tired of the anti-Semitism spewed by prominent blacks.

And then, in an attempt to put out the fire, Louis Farrakhan shows up with dry leaves and a gas can. He proceeded to not only threaten Coleman during a radio broadcast but then also issued a warning to Jews in general that if they "harmed this brother [Jackson] . . . it would be the last one they harmed." Nice damage control, dick.

A few weeks later, Jackson admitted saying it, and apologized in a New Hampshire synagogue (smart choice, as there are only nine Jews in the entire state). This was not by any means an isolated incident; Jesse had a history of bellyaching about the Jews. And he still ran for president twice because the Democrats forgave him. This double standard of forgiveness for racist speech is enraging, although not surprising. Can you imagine if a prominent white leader had referred to a city like New Orleans as "Niggertown"? They'd be drummed out of public prominence faster than you can say Trent Lott. A white leader would never say something so inflammatory about such a fine city; they'd simply wait until it was flooded and then do nothing about it for five days.

My problem with Jesse Jackson has nothing to do with the fact that he's repeatedly made an asshole out of himself publicly. I give less than a shit about his feelings concerning Jews (or any other white people, for that matter). It's just that knowing his history, and considering all the accusations about him lying, one would think that whenever others are accused of making inappropriate racial remarks, he would think of glass houses, rocks, and things of that ilk. But he doesn't. He refuses to miss an opportunity to stick his ugly face in front of a microphone and demand apologies and firings. He then demands that blacks be inserted into openings that *he* helped create by whining like a hypersensitive cunt. Once, just once, I want to see a black leader, elected or otherwise, stick up for the white guy in a racial situation.

A fine example would be the Duke rape case. As everyone remembers, a black stripper (who turned out to be a lying twat) accused the Duke lacrosse team of gang-raping her at a party. She was never raped. The boys gave her tips to play the spoons on her clitoris.

Simply because of the racial component, Jesse the knee-jerk-reactionary asshole announced that the Rainbow Coalition would pay her college tuition *even if her accusations were proven false.* God, what a douchebag. Now that her accusations have indeed been proven false, I'm curious if the Rainbow Coalition followed through and helped this misunderstood enchantress finish school. Or, did she go back to accepting rolled-up dead presidents via her cervix? On a side note, I can't tell you how tickled I am that he named his organization the Rainbow Coalition shortly before the image of the rainbow was hijacked by every gay organization from San Francisco to Miami.

The case that really makes me want to kick the good reverend in the balls is, of course, Imus. Not only did this predictable fuckhead call for Imus's firing but he organized and participated in protests. At a horribly attended rally outside NBC in Chicago, he said, "NBC must choose between Imus and the rest of us." Who's the rest of us—you and the other fifty disgruntled, unemployed jerk-offs blocking traffic? But, because a few of the advertisers pulled out (what else is new—advertisers are notorious cowards), NBC canceled the simulcast of the show. I'm surprised NBC didn't appease black activists by replacing Imus's show with a daily four-hour marathon of white businessmen deep-tonguing Jesse Jackson's and Al Sharpton's assholes.

Next stop on the Jesse the Hypocritical Scumbag Tour was CBS. Jackson called the firing "A victory for public decency. No one should use the public airwaves to transmit racial or sexual degradation." I wonder when Jesse became such an expert on public decency; perhaps he had an epiphany while sticking his dick in one of his aides during an extramarital affair he was having? Is that what happened, Jess? While you were blowing a load in her and fathering a child out of wedlock, did you suddenly realize that you were, through proxy, degrading your wife sexually? Did you then realize that made you an expert on the subject of sexual degradation?

When he realized it was about to go public, Jackson released a statement saying, "I fully accept responsibility, and I am truly sorry for my actions." Gee whiz, doesn't that sound familiar? What older white gentleman was saying that recently? Lucky for you there wasn't some self-righteous, self-important piece of shit gunning for you and forcing people to remove you from your job. Oh, that's right . . . no one can remove you from your job because, technically, no one knows what the fuck your job is. (And even if anyone was gunning for you, you could have just blamed cheating on your wife on the dirty, awful Jews.)

To be completely honest, I don't exactly hate Jesse Jackson; I just think he's an asshole. At best, I find him to be misguided; at worst, a blithering idiot. There is some element of sincerity in what he does, which is a rare quality in a megalomaniac. Undeniably, he did help secure the freedom of some captured U.S. servicemen in Syria and Cuba, regardless of how unpopular his trips were with the State Department. See, you thought this was going to be an essay beating the shit out of the good reverend, but it turned out to be pretty fair and balanced, didn't it?

POSITIVE THINGS ABOUT JESSE JACKSON:

- He has, to my knowledge, never had anal sex with anyone under the age of ten.

- He steadfastly refuses to shit his pants.

- He refuses to filter money from his charity in order to pay for shit in his personal life, despite numerous accusations of doing so.

- Jesse does what Jesse wants to do—like offering to pay the tuition of a proven liar who shows her cunt for a living, as opposed to contributing to the defense fund of the three men whose lives she attempted to ruin.

- As an act of rebellion, he has refused to master the white man's language. Instead, he chooses to communicate in what sounds like a combination of Swahili and Bell's palsy.

- When someone fixes something in a nontraditional way, Jesse will joke that they "Sharpton-rigged" it.

- Not only did he fuck a woman behind his wife's back but he also kept it real and decided not to pull out or wear a condom.

- He decided to run for president twice, despite the fact that the Hillside Strangler had a more realistic shot of getting the Democratic nomination.

- He has refused to blame Jews for sickle-cell anemia, Hurricane Katrina, or the Indonesian tsunami.

- When hit with a desire to cut off Barack Obama's balls, or refer to blacks as niggers, he has the courtesy to whisper these thoughts into a live microphone on the most conservative news channel in the country.

- Hopefully, his blood test results.

My Main Man, K-Fed

I OBVIOUSLY risk alienating much of my audience by even presenting the possibility that I'm going to bad-mouth rude boy Kevin Federline. Of course, I hated him at first, just like everyone else in the free world. Why did I hate him, you ask? Very simply—I just didn't get it.

My epiphany came one magical Sunday afternoon. I remember it as if it were yesterday; I was sitting on the toilet, forehead sweating profusely. My eyes were slammed shut, and I was attempting to force out a shit the size of a rolling pin. Progress was slow. The log was behaving so stubbornly, I almost contacted a hostage negotiator to talk it out. I even attempted using a little toilet stool I have, which, when my feet are placed on it, raises my knees to chest level (this is supposed to be the body's natural position when evacuating). Nothing worked. I dozed off at least four times, waking up furious because I was missing the *M*A*S*H* marathon on Channel 5. Music began drifting in from the other room, and my numb leg began tapping involuntarily to the beat. It was Kevin, singing his first big hit, "PopoZão." My asshole, in the midst of this realization, parted like the Red Sea and dropped something that theoretically could have tumbled out of the Enola Gay in 1945. His greatness suddenly hit me like a ton of vomit.

Sure, we all love to dance the night away to hit songs like "PopoZão" and "Lose Control." Yet people don't seem to want to credit the musical architect behind these auditory masterpieces. Miraculously, the public rejected "PopaZão" as a single, and K-Fed was forced to pull it from his debut album, *Playing with Fire* (which is what you're doing if you tangle with K-Fed, IMHO). The album cover is super cool; it features Kevin staring toughly into the camera, wearing a dress shirt with the sleeves rolled up and a tie that has been loosened up top. The intense look on his face says it all: the man is ready for action. A deck of playing cards in his hands, a drink in front of him, and a cigarette smoldering in the ashtray. Playing with fire? You're goddamn right you are.

The big get-off of *Playing with Fire* is "Lose Control," destined to be an anthem among young people. It not only has a beat that makes it an undeniable toe-tapper but the lyrics are also powerful and almost make you feel like you're a member of K-Fed's posse. He raps about his Lamborghini, his tuxedo, and Vegas craps tables—things that are all synonymous with Kevin.

The main reason the public has overwhelmingly rejected Kevin, aside from being threatened by his ability to rap like nobody's business, is anger over what's happened to Britney Spears. John Q. Public blames K-Fed for her plummet from iconic sex symbol to white trashy tabloid joke of the day. And, in a way, the public's right. Miss Hoity-Toity was flying high on top of the world when a certain background dancer caught her eye. Their first night out was the stuff of fairy tales. She and Kevin put on his-and-her piss bags and went on a romantic outing, which started in a Waffle House and ended in a six-hour cow-tipping marathon.

Well, wouldn't you know it . . . ten minutes after ol' donkey dick gets a hold of her, she's costarring in a reality show and slurring like Dick Clark after a pint of vodka. This, in addition to suddenly speaking in a slow, moronic Southern drawl. Britney's superstar Halloween mask had been removed and revealed her to be nothing more than a hotter, more fuckable version of Larry the Cable Guy. Like it or not, K-Fed had deep-dicked the phoniness right out of her. And he promptly began further wrecking that sexy image by refusing to dump loads anywhere but inside her womb. His momma didn't raise no dummy; after every fuck, he'd push her legs back to her ears and hermetically seal her pussy with duct tape and grout. Kevin was on a mission to knock this bizz-itch up, and—I remind you to reference the *Playing with Fire* album cover to understand—when this stud sets his mind on a mission, that mission gets done. Kevin the Destroyer didn't waste an ounce of semen for three years. He was so intent on knocking her up that when she was on the road he'd masturbate into a Baggie, wait until she came home, and then squeeze it into her pussy like space food. Attaboy, Kev!

For the world premiere of "Lose Control," Britney introduced Kevin at the 2006 Teen Choice Awards. She came out in a pink dress looking extremely pregnant thanks to a very potent batch of K-Fed seeds. You could see how jealous she was, because when she introduced him, she had the same look on her face a woman gets when a dragonfly has landed on her clit. Kevin burst out looking funky-fresh and sharp in a white tank top, white jacket, and appropriately tilted white baseball cap. He really brought down the house! His dance moves were superlative; he truly captured the urban experience. A lot of people bashed his performance, saying that he's nothing more than a dull, no-talent wigger, that he's an embarrassment, and that he has the rapping ability of an autistic with a mouth full of ice who has just bitten his tongue. I was not one of those people.

His album debuted at number 151 on the Billboard 200, selling an estimated 6,500 copies in the first week alone. Not too shabby. The second week, sales dropped off a bit, down to 1,200. I attribute the low sales figures to stores being sold out and people downloading his music illegally.

To give credit where it's due, that Federline kid must be one heck of a fuck. Before he came along, Britney was floating on air, virtually unstoppable. No sooner does Kevin get those baby-fat legs pinned behind her head than he proceeds to fuck the career right out of her. One minute she's on MTV making out with Madonna, the next she's drunk driving and juggling a baby while her pussy fishes around for change under the seat.

The one thing K-Fed did that I didn't like was get involved with professional wrestling. I was on eggshells for months, terrified he would get hurt. John Cena (another white guy who has an authentic grip on urban slang and dialect) picked Kevin up and slammed him onto the ground. I was beside myself. Hopefully, that silly chapter in his life is over so he can get back to what he does best—writing hit music.

There is obviously no need to list improvement suggestions for Kevin, but there are a few things I'd love to see him do, which would make him even cooler in my eyes (ha, like that's possible).

- Sing more ballads. You're going to eventually hurt those golden pipes doing all that hard-hitting rapping. We don't need you burning out before you're thirty, buddy.

- *More acting!* I'd love to see you play a streetwise thug, or perhaps a tourist who is kidnapped by an Amish pimp and forced to suck dick behind a butter churn.

- Start your own line of designer condoms. Have little holes prepoked in the tip and dollar signs drawn down the length of them.

- Create an involved, highly produced stage show around "PopoZáo," the way Styx did with "Mr. Roboto."

- Gather up Vanilla Ice, Marky Mark & the Funky Bunch, and Jim Norton from 1986, and start up a festival called Wiggerpalooza.

He's Fat . . . He's Phony . . . He's Maxwell!

maxwell /maks wel/

(noun)

a shower of water: *a daily maxwell*

A jet of liquid applied to part of the body for cleansing or medicinal purposes.

A device for washing out the vagina as a contraceptive measure.

(verb /trans./)

to spray or shower with water.

/intrans./

to use a maxwell as a method of contraception.

With the exception of fifty people in Ohio, everyone reading this is wondering, *Who the fuck is Maxwell?* Exactly. He's a morbidly obese afternoon radio hack in Cleveland who suffers from sleep apnea. One of these absolute jerk-offs trying to sound like a gravelly gritty rock star who "tells it like it is." In reality, he's a bald prick who wears thick welder's glasses and has a goatee, which makes him look like Donald Pleasence. He's the quintessential slappable fat nerd trying to sound like a hard-ass.

Of course, his real name isn't Maxwell. That's just the tough-as-nails moniker he made up for himself. His untamable out-of-control alter ego, if you will. His real name is Benjamin Bornstein. Doesn't have quite the same ring, does it? Chicks with big tits would never want to do shots with Benjamin Bornstein. But when Maxwell walks into the party . . . "woooh-hoooo! Bottoms up, motherfuckers!!"

To match his phony made-up radio name, he uses a phony made-up radio voice. If you've spent more than five minutes flipping through radio stations in any town in the country, you've heard a carbon copy of this generic, run-of-the-mill pole smoker. You know the sound: it's that overly inflected dragged-out-words voice with a manufactured scratchiness to it. I love radio guys who have so little faith in what they're actually saying that they need to concentrate on bullshit inflection.

And in the style of the true jerk-off, he has a catchphrase. Yes, a fucking catchphrase. It's enough to make you puke. After he pontificates about something, to put real punctuation on it, he ends the segment by saying, "And punt." (Actually, when hearing it in his fraudulent, dime-a-dozen, schlocky radio voice, it's, "*Ayand puhhnt.*") The first time I heard it, I assumed he was attempting irony. No one, and I mean *no one*, could actually think that's an edgy, in-your-face thing to say. *And punt*?? Are you fucking kidding me? I don't even I know what it means. Guess what you said is unfollowable, huh . . . your opponent better just punt? Or is it "a real man has just made a definitive statement"? Whatever it means, it's the worst example of a verbal exclamation point I've ever heard. I'd respect him more if he said, "Talk to the hand" or just stole, "And that's the name of that tune!" from Baretta.

At one point, and I'm not sure if he still does, he had AND PUNT T-shirts on his website (you know, for all the guys who pump their fists in the air when he says it). It makes a great gift for the guy who has everything, including incest fantasies and a mullet.

Now, the reason I am even mentioning this prematurely bald shit stain is because he started bad-mouthing Opie, Anthony, and me. Like most everyone else in the country, we had never heard of this cunt-faced walrus. We got audio of him saying we used to be funny, but we're just not anymore. "They're just nahhhhtttt fuhhnnyy." Then he starts telling his sidekick, Fatso #2, that he's funnier than me. Bornstein starts telling Fatso #2 that I'm overrated, and that he is funnier on the air than I am. "Pound for pound, you're funnier than him." (Paywwnd for paywwnd, you're fuhhnnier 'n him.) This idiot, this poor fucking slob he works with, starts putting on his "Aw, shucks, little ole me?" routine and I wanted to vomit. I was genuinely embarrassed for him.

Fatso #2 finally gave in, admitted that he was, indeed, pound for pound more amusing than me (I imagine he said this after looking down and sheepishly kicking the floor). You easily manipulated trite *asshole*. I would never, under any circumstances, attempt to boast that I was funnier than someone else. It's douche chill-inducing. Only people who truly aren't funny think like that. Not surprising though. You're a wannabe sidekick on a wannabe show.

Thus far, my favorite moment of the fight we're having with this dick is undoubtedly the time he finally talked about us giving out his real name on the air. Of course we didn't just say "Benjamin Bornstein," we mocked the awfulness of it. It got to him. He tried to explain it away like it was no big deal. While it wasn't a secret of the Manhattan Project magnitude, it's still something he definitely didn't want getting out. Would you?

He started off by saying that giving out his real name isn't exactly a coup, which we never claimed it was. We were simply trying to inform his listeners that this humdrum asshole puts on the equivalent of an emotional Halloween costume when he goes on the air. It's hard for me to respect a guy who isn't even open about his own name.

He continued, "Snoop Dogg's real name is Calvin Broadus. Do you hate him now?" I laughed out loud when he said that. He actually compared himself to Snoop Dogg. Snoop is an ex–gang banger, a pimp, has been arrested on gun and drug charges, and is arguably the most successful hip-hop artist in the country. Benjamin Bornstein is a dull, relatively unknown afternoon radio guy who looks like Detective Frank Cannon. Do you honestly think that you and Snoop are two peas in a pod, you fucking idiot?

It was really interesting listening to this douchebag (deewwche baaig) criticize my HBO special. He was saying how the first batch of comedy from me was great, but now I'm just not funny. (The fact that he used the phrase "batch of comedy" goes to show what a stupid cunt he is. Nice terminology, you fucking old lady. Why not just tell me to respect my elders and then insist I put a sweater on because it's chilly outside.) I have never tried to argue with someone for not thinking I'm funny—that's completely subjective and there are plenty of people who will always think I suck. Fair enough. But to say my older material is better just shows what a novice, what a *spectator*, he really is. Which one of my older bits do you mean, fatboy? When I used to open my set by saying, "I hate when people ask what exit I'm from in New Joisey, and I reply 'Exit one!'" and stick up my middle finger? Is that one of the gems you're referring to?

Of course I realize that shitting on my own material is counterproductive. But I am not naïve enough to think the stuff I did for the first ten years of my career is better than the stuff I wrote about Imus, Islam-a-phobia, or the lie of political correctness, etc. Comedians become better over the years, not worse. But why would I expect a fat slob who needs air forced down his throat so he doesn't choke on his own tongue at night to understand that?

Then he starts babbling about how my material is shock value.

I'm always amazed when some unimaginative dunce uses this term. I see comedy in a completely different light. I try to say the funniest thing possible and am colossally irritated if people find it shocking. I don't comprehend being shocked by humor. We are all adults and I detest this "little girl" mentality and reaction to it. The beautiful irony of this jealous scumbag calling me shock value is that on his website he has a section with all of the girls he likes called "Maxwell's Whores." Wow maaahhhnnn, how extreme! How rock and roll of you! "They're all whores, man, and these are the ones I'd like to fuck . . . yeaahhh!!" But *I'm* shock value? Fuck you and your made-up-voice radio persona, you fraudulent cornball.

In the midst of the effortless pummeling we were giving this jackass, I decided to go perform in Cleveland. That's how little respect I had for any influence he thought he wielded. Cleveland has always been great to me, and I was able to sell out two shows at the House of Blues. I cannot tell you how satisfying it was to have more than eight hundred people a show screaming, "Maxwell's a cunt!" and "Nice apnea, dick," and mocking his voice. Literally, the entire audience was screaming "Nahhhht fuuuhhnnnyy" in unison. How do you like them apples? I walked into your yard, by my lonesome, and pissed all over your front door. Cleveland is supposed to be *your* town, and they hate your fucking guts. People actually showed up in homemade shirts.

BENJAMIN BORNSTEIN IS A FAT CUNT. I love this shirt so much I didn't even notice her wonderful tits at first.

Another true sign that someone is completely unqualified to discuss comedy is when he starts putting restrictions on what content is funny and acceptable, and what isn't. Louis C.K. called in to *The Benjamin Bornstein Show* and was discussing watching his kids when his wife was out. He made a joke that if he didn't watch them properly they might fall out the window like Eric Clapton's stupid kid (I am paraphrasing and, of course, destroying what was a genuinely funny, off-the-cuff line). Bornstein the Jizzbag immediately says how Louis shouldn't make fun of that ("Thayts nahht fuhhny") and then laughs. Make up your mind, you chemically imbalanced queer.

Or, how about this—how about you stop trying to be a community leader in the morality parade and just let funny people do what they do while you do what you do, which is stand on the sidelines and be a good little (*fat*) laughing machine: Toward the end of the call, Louis mentions that he's looking forward to doing the Buffalo gig and Bornstein has to tell him that he's based out of Cleveland. How'd that feel, you fucking nobody? How'd it feel to know Louis had no goddamn idea who you are? Kind of embarrassing, huh, rock star?

And then after they nicely wrap up the call (thanks a lot for calling, blah blah blah), that coward starts to trash Louis for real. He starts in with more of his what-content-is-appropriate dogshit and then starts blasting Louis for a joke on his HBO special that Louis never did. You made up a joke and attributed it to Louis just to make your bullshit point, you fucking rube. You lying cunt. Truth be told, I think what really got to you deep down, Benny, was that Louis inadvertently showed you exactly how big of an impact you've made in the radio world. He had no idea who you were, he had no idea where you were broadcasting from, and neither does most of the country.

That must be pretty upsetting, huh, baby boy? You must be tired of sitting on the sidelines for most of the game. Tired of having to explain to friends and family why you are where you are after all these years. Honestly, Bornstein, I don't blame you for being bitter. This is probably not the way you saw it going down when you started. You probably never envisioned having a family depend on you while you were still virtually unrecognizable in the business. Never saw your ass-kicking self taking a call from a brilliant comic who, in the end, humiliated you in front of your audience by inadvertently showing them what a fucking non-player you really are. And the reason no one knows who you are is very simple: you suck.

Knowing I'd be trashing him in this book, I needed to bite the bullet and force myself to listen to some of his material. I went online and subjected myself to this remarkably unfunny louse because I wanted to be able to hear for myself and quote him accurately. The bits I heard weren't at all offensive, with the exception of the fact that this fucking cluck was once again attempting to be amusing. Benjamin, and I mean this without rancor—you're just not a funny guy. Stop trying to be a comedic force—you aren't, and never will be. You're an envious, fledgling hack who probably talks dirty to a chick in that hokey radio voice while he fucks her. "Thaayyt's riiight baayybee, take thayat caahhhhkk." And how long do you have to beg before they're willing to call you Maxwell in the sack, instead of Benjamin or Piggy Boy? In order to cum, women must have to close their eyes and pretend you're a hundred pounds lighter and syndicated to at least three cities. And syndication is obviously right around the corner with bits like these. Here are a couple of the well-written, impeccably delivered masterpieces I stumbled upon:

- A phone call where a counselor was calling for one of his patients. Apparently, the counselor accidentally called the radio show instead, and madness ensued! Whoever answered the phone said the guy whom the counselor was looking for had killed himself. The counselor was saddened, then the prankster laughed, and said, "Just kidding," and hung up on him. Now, if this call was real, then he's not only an asshole (SHOCK VALUE! SHOCK VALUE!) but also a stupid asshole, because putting a person on the radio without their knowledge is illegal and an FCC violation. If it's fake, and it more than likely was, he should fucking kill himself for relying on made-up "phony phone calls." Fucking zoo-crew hack. My AIDS jokes—bad! Louie's joke about a kid falling out the window—bad. Your joke about a guy who is trying to straighten his life out, who has a relapse and kills himself, *made to a guy who was actually trying* to *help him*—acceptable? See what I mean? You phony scumbag.

- Another hilarious gem I listened to online was "Maxwell Films: Spending Too Much Time at the Strip Club." Now put on your laughing hats, here's one of the rib-tickling lines he came up with, "You ever notice that every year when you have your taxes done, the preparer asks if you gave any money to charity last year and you reply, 'Yeah, I gave money to charity . . . and Dominique . . . and Sasha.'" Huh? Oh, wait a minute . . . I get it: Charity is the name of a stripper! Hahahaha! See, at first, I thought that he meant he gave to a charitable organization, but then, once he mentioned other girls' names, LOL, I realized where he was going with it! Hahaha. I *love* wordplay jokes. I'm looking *this* way, then you come at me *that* way! You gave money to *Charity.* I'll bet you did, you sly dog, you!

- And at the risk of driving even more listeners to this radio laugh-a-thon, I'll give you the next joke from the bit. Now breathe deep and get ready, because here comes another hard-hitting line: "Finally, one day you have an epiphany and realize, yes, you have been spending too much time at the strip club, it was apparent that time they kicked you out of Applebee's and said, 'You ain't welcome back until you learn how to put the tip on the table like everyone else.'" Wait a minute . . . now, Benjamin . . . were you putting the tips in between the waitresses' breasts?? No you didn't! Hahahaha, no wonder they threw you out! They can't run a legitimate business with nuts like you throwing dollar bills around all willy-nilly! Gee whiz, when you said you spend too much time at the strip club, you weren't kidding!

And to clarify: I understand the last hunk of shit line I quoted from him seems like one long run-on sentence. That's because that's how he delivered it. It figures that apnea-ridden cunt wouldn't have the sense of timing enough to slow down or break up the sentence. And this entire bit is delivered in Jackie Gleason's "Reginald Van Gleason" voice. Fucking asshole.

Now some of you may be surmising that I'm only accusing this fat load of having a sucky show just because he bad-mouthed us. Not true. I accuse his show of being unlistenable because it is. We've been in plenty of on-air radio fights before; I wouldn't say the same about all of the shows we've fought.

An old rule in radio is to never reference the competition by name, lest your audience checks them out and falls in love with their show, effectively abandoning you. To me, that is typical cowardly program director bullshit. One of the things that bothered Bornstein the most was when we played audio of his bits on air and destroyed him. The bits stunk (not unlike the banal rubbish I quoted in this chapter), and we allowed them to speak for themselves. They were pseudoedgy garbage.

I encourage you to check out his show. I encourage you to go on YouTube and listen to the shitty bits he has on it. If you actually think this rancorous show is funnier than the *Opie & Anthony* show, then I encourage you to turn the dial permanently, and listen to him instead. And then, of course, to kill yourself.

As of this writing, we are just about done with Benjamin Bornstein.

NICE APNEA, DICK. Thank you, madam. I couldn't have said it better myself.

Our fans (the Pests) have kicked the living shit out of him. They hijacked his MySpace page and tortured him with calls so badly he couldn't go to the phones on his own radio show.

And all we had to do was play audio of his show and allow the shittiness of it to speak for itself. And he's certainly not straightforward enough to admit the volume of calls he's gotten, or the amount of problems our fans have caused him. That would require being honest with his listeners. I wouldn't hold my breath waiting for honesty from a guy who uses a fake name and fake voice. The closest he could come to admitting his frustration was when he went on the air and started whining, "I don't know why they care so much what we say about them—we're just a small local radio show." You fat, destined-for-mediocrity fucking baby. He wants to talk shit unprovoked, then wonders why we respond? *Why are you picking on us, we're just a smaaaall shooooow.* If we ignore it, we're pussies; if we attack you, we're bullies? I guess we just can't win, can we, Benji? And it won't surprise me if he says something equally predictable about me wasting pages on him in my book. In actuality, I rather enjoyed writing this chapter; it was quite cathartic. And I certainly wouldn't consider it a waste, Benjamin—you're well worth the effort. Ayand Puhhnt.

TO AVOID LOOKING HARSH AND UNYIELDING, I'VE DECIDED TO INCLUDE A LIST OF TEN THINGS BENJAMIN BORNSTEIN CAN DO TO WIPE THE SLATE CLEAN WITH ME

1. Commit suicide.

2–10. See number one.

Shitty Celebrity Couple Names

WHEN DID this "cutesy-wootsey" celebrity name game begin? People commonly point to Bill and Hillary Clinton. The term "Billary" became common when referring to the First Couple since he was elected President, yet we always got the impression she had attached little fishhooks to his balls to control him. This moniker came about not long after Bill first got into the White House because people weren't used to such an irritatingly ambitious First Lady. We had gotten used to Barbara Bush and Nancy Reagan, two First Ladies whose only ambition was to help their husbands make it through their respective terms without shitting their presidential pants.

Nancy was attacked for her "Just Say No" slogan because people thought it was an elitist, out-of-touch answer for kids facing drugs. She later admitted she was quoted out of context, and had simply been answering Dan Rather's question, "What do you do when Ronnie tries to stick it in your ass?" (Ronnie was a notorious hiney licker. He once explained to Mike Wallace that his jellybean obsession began when he found they effectively removed the vinegary aftertaste of Nancy's asshole.)

The first of these repulsive combo-names has to be Desi Arnaz and Lucille Ball, combining to make Desilu Productions. (The original production company name of I'll Cheat All I Want, You Carrot-Headed

Bitch Productions was deemed too long to effectively fit on business cards.) Lucy and Desi created the three-camera shoot in a sitcom, an idea they stole from William Frawley, who used the three-camera shoot to make films of himself masturbating into Vivian Vance's flowered hats.

2002 proved to be wonderful for revitalizing the combo name when Ben Affleck met gifted thespian Jennifer Lopez on the set of Oscar-nominated *Gigli* (a quaint little film about a mobster, a retard, and a lesbian). It was considered something of a success, costing only $54 million to make and pulling in an impressive $7 million worldwide. Al Pacino even had a part in this one. I didn't see the film, but I heard he played a once-great actor whoring himself for what amounts to stolen money.

Let's forget Pacino for a moment, and that godawful Emilio Estevez wig he's been wearing for the past ten years. This is about Ben and Jennifer, or as I prefer to call them, Bennifer. Not sure why they chose Bennifer, when there were other juicy choices: Jaffleck, Jennaleck, Jenniben, and Blopez. Or simply Bunt (for Ben and Cunt). After a whirlwind relationship filled with mystery and intrigue, they broke up in 2004 after Ben walked in and caught her masturbating with a rolled-up Marc Anthony poster.

As of this writing, the truly revolting one is Brangelina. This winning combination is of course the fusion of Angelina Jolie and Brad Pitt. Our spies tell us they fell in love on the set of *Mr. & Mrs. Smith*, a drama about a sexy, dominant woman of moderate skills who suckers a teen idol into carrying her bags and adopting the equivalent of a UN peacekeeping force. (They are rumored to be building a barn to store their adopted children in, while their biological children sleep in the main house in a straw-filled manger.)

The aggravating aspect of these two is their constant attempts at social and political relevance. Endless praise is heaped on them for all the charity work they do, and at the risk of being hailed a naysayer, their charity work is shit. Starving people, AIDS babies, global warming, and a few other easy picks: Who gives a hoot? Every asshole on the planet cares about hungry babies and a hole in the ozone; think out of the box a little. How about a real humanitarian effort, like giving a few ugly guys a chance to fuck Angelina? Or, maybe Brad Pitt takes a girl with a harelip to her high school prom. At the end of the night, he gives her a kiss on her balloon-knotted lips and pretends not to throw up in his own mouth. A few of Angelina's current charities:

- Goodwill Ambassador for the UN Refugee Agency. This agency protects refugees who are bolting from their home countries and coming to the United States. Not impressive. Anyone who can float over here on a screen door doesn't need anything from Angelina (other than her collagen lips wrapped around their weary, well-traveled penises).

- She's on the board of advisors for the Yale Haiti Foundation, which uses art and music to bring goodwill to Haiti. Another clunker. You want to bring goodwill to Haiti, let's start with some hepatitis-free drinking water. Mind your fucking beeswax, whitey, and let Wyclef Jean worry about Haiti.

- Allowed *People* magazine to print her first pregnant photos for a $500,000 donation. Well hot-diggity-dog! How about she keeps the fat photos and sends out a few shots of Brad emptying his balls into her?

- Between *People* and *Hello!* magazines, Brangelina were paid approximately $10 million for first pictures of their biological daughter (which is twice what Woody Allen offered for the shots).

- Has visited Darfur, Sierra Leone, Cambodia, and Tanzania. Whoop-dee-fucking-doo. Paid vacations. And she donated $1 million to help out. Women in Darfur don't need money, they need clitorises. If Angelina really wanted to help, she'd have packed three million clits in her carry-on bag.

By far the most irritating thing they've done for attention was moving to New Orleans. Their reason, according to them, was to shed more light on the plight of the people living there. Bullshit. They've adopted so many fucking kids, they needed a bigger house, and figured they could get a good deal on the Super Dome. And then this stupid rumor started that Brad got a tattoo of the New Orleans levee system on his back. At least that's what he claims. Could just as easily be scratch marks Angelina left there as she held on while giving him a lesson with the strap-on.

TomKat!

If you didn't know better, you'd think Tom Cruise was now fucking Kat Williams. Or perhaps you wouldn't think that. Perhaps it just comes to my mind as a result of jerking off to it. The Kat is short for *Dawson's Creek* star Katie Holmes, who met Tom when he had her come to his office to read for a part. (Jesus, that old gag. I knew it worked, but on Katie Holmes?) The fact that I just wrote the equivalent of "But seriously, folks . . ." then explained the real origin of TomKat is reason enough to bury a cinder block in my frontal lobe.

The great part of this relationship is that it marked the end of Tom's impeccable, untouchable image. For more than twenty years, he was this charming sex symbol that every woman wanted to fuck and every guy wanted to hang out with (if only to lick his fingers clean at the end of the day). Then . . . something happened.

One day we all turned on *Oprah*—I didn't even know Tom was on that day. I was expecting a heavily promoted Dr. Phil segment on how to gently tell your spouse that her asshole smells like onion soup—and saw Tom Cruise jumping up and down on the couch. You could almost feel the entire country sigh at once and mumble, "Oh, no, he's an asshole." An almost twenty-five-year love affair was replaced with instant irritation. People intuitively understood that seeing him jumping up and down like a boob was seeing him totally naked. This was him, it was who he was. Not an evil guy, not a piece of shit, just a goddamn fool. What was supposed to be an "endearing peek" into his boyish enthusiasm for his new love instead made all of us want to quietly lay our heads under a tractor wheel.

For years, people have known Tom is a Scientologist, and most of us didn't give a shit. I've heard some bizarre things about Scientologists, but as long as they weren't bothering me, old Tommy-boy could waste his time anywhere he wanted on Sunday mornings. But once he started very publicly debating people and espousing his views, we all started looking at one another out of the corners of our eyes: "Oh, no, he's not just an asshole, he's fucking nuts."

It started when he criticized Brooke Shields for taking antidepressants to treat postpartum depression. That was the beginning of the end for Tom. None of us were comfortable seeing Brooke criticized. We love her. Who among us can resist jerking off to her scenes in *Pretty Baby*? Or even to some of her later work, when she was over the hill, as in *The Blue Lagoon* and *Endless Love*?

Brooke responded by releasing a harsh statement that said, in part, "Tom Cruise is just as off base as he can be, and can go jump in the lake as far as I'm concerned. I say, nerts to Tom!" In conjunction with the release of the statement, she sent a suicide bomber to Tom's house disguised as the Sasquatch. Tom, smelling a rat, attacked the intruder with a flame-thrower, and then forced him to watch *Lions for Lambs*. Then, upping the ante, he hired five Mexicans to shit on Brooke's porch and set it on fire. Katie Holmes attempted to quiet the storm, but everyone looked at her and asked, "Who the fuck are you again?" so she sat down. Brooke alleg-edly plastered Tom's neighborhood with photocopies of her asshole, which forced Tom to end the feud by sending Brooke a basket of baby gifts, which was rumored to include plastic Baggies, thumbtacks, and lead-paint chips. According to sources, they've made up and have both agreed to perform in blackface during their much-anticipated remake of *Cornbread, Earl and Me*.

CELEBRITY COMBO NAMES I WOULD APPROVE OF:

- Dalanski—Dakota Fanning and Roman Polanski
- Faget—Farrah Fawcett and Bob Saget
- Killit—pre-1984 Keisha Knight Pulliam and R. Kelly
- Dykalina—K. D. Lang and Rosie O'Donnell
- Spook—Britney Spears and Dane Cook

People I Wanted to Kill on Sight: Part Three

- The girl who emailed me a picture of her fat vagina this afternoon. I intended on getting quite a bit of writing done today; instead I jerked off until my dick looked like a burn victim. I then proceeded to write exactly three sentences, including this one.

- Bob Kelly once again, this time for attempting to give workout advice. We were both shirtless in the gym locker room, both relatively disgraceful looking. This head case looks me up and down, and gives a detailed report on what's wrong with my torso. He then begins giving step-by-step instructions on exactly what exercises I need to be doing. All this while standing there wrapped in a towel, resembling a goateed hippopotamus. He allows himself the leeway to do something this psychotic by giving a shitty disclaimer first, "Look, dude, I know I'm a mess, but . . ." Oh, do you really, Dr. Phil? You know you're a mess? Then you must also know how badly I want to burn your balls with a curling iron. How about next time you end that statement properly: "Look, dude, I know I'm a mess . . . so I'm going to keep my fucking mouth shut."

- The Stone Temple Pilots. I took the noon train to Boston today with Op and Ant to attend the River Rave. We were supposed to interview the band, and then Op and Ant would announce them at the show. So we sit around in the dressing room, then, of course, we get the word that STP canceled the interview. Why? Because their overly coddled, pussy lead singer isn't at the venue yet. I heard he was an hour late going onstage the night before, now tonight he can't show up for an interview. Fuck him. So he finally shows up and skips into his tour bus. Now the stage managers are telling us to "clear the backstage area at the request of the Stone Temple Pilots." "But we have all-access passes from the station who's presenting the event." "Doesn't matter, the band wants everybody out." Do they? Well, I want the band to not be whiny, typical prima donna rock star faggots. Perhaps we can find a compromise? Honestly, I don't know if it was Scott Weiland or the entire band, but I'll blame it on him. We've interviewed a couple of those guys and they were very cool; he seems like one of those pathetic celebrities who needs constant care and attention or he gets his tampon in a bunch. Musicians in general are pains in the ass. Comics are easy; we show up at the gig and don't need anything more than bottled water, luncheon meat, and a dark corner to possibly get blown in after the show.

Conclusion

IS THERE really a need for a conclusion to this book? I don't think so, and I'm not just saying that because I'm way over deadline and too lazy to write one. But I think it speaks for itself. It's a couple of hundred pages of bile—emotional vomiting, if you will. And it felt great, I mean really terrific. Building up hatred is the kind of thing that just sits in you, eats away at you, and it's unhealthy. People don't have heart attacks because they don't exercise, they have heart attacks because every time they see that asshole neighbor across the street they're driven mad with a desire to stick a knife in him. It's the resentments that kill us. And, they say, we're only as sick as our secrets. Letting out that poison is the only true road to happiness. On the surface, it may appear that I'm just a venomous prick who had nothing to do for the past six months and needed some cash. (Which is, coincidentally, exactly how it appears below the surface.)

So, thank you for reading this, unless you're one of the people I attacked, in which case, thank you for just being you.

Acknowledgments

MOM, DAD, Tracy, Nick, and all of my aunts, uncles, and cousins. Thank you for always making eye contact with me at family functions.

Opie & Anthony, not only for being my friends, but for getting me up so fucking early every day. And of course, for being there for me and supporting me every step of the way. (I should have a cock shoved in my mouth for writing that.)

Club Soda Kenny, for always making sure I'm awake on time, and never rolling over on me when we sleep.

David Steinberg, Jonathan Brandstein, Pete Pappalardo, Dennis Arfa, Larry Brezner, Robert Eatman, and the staffs of MBST, AGI, and Robert Eatman Enterprises. Thanks for not only furthering my career, but for not stealing my money.

All of my friends at HBO; Nancy Geller, Nina Rosenstein, Aaron Spina, Richard Pepler, and the people behind the scenes who made *Down and Dirty with Jim Norton* possible.

All the comics who did *Down and Dirty*, especially Andrew Dice Clay, Artie Lange, Bill Burr, and Patrice Oneal.

Lemmy, for being such a great addition to *Down and Dirty*, as well as for crooning my favorite love songs. Also Dixon, for helping us work through all the details.

Acknowledgments

Lisa Kussell at BWR, for bamboozling people into thinking I'm worth interviewing.

Lydia Wills, you're an excellent literary agent. How you convinced anyone to pay for this horseshit is beyond me.

Tricia Boczkowski, my editor, for never asking me to change jokes because they're too mean. Your encouragement has helped me be all the literary scumbag I can be.

Jen Bergstrom, for once again funding my escort addiction by okaying this deal.

Greg Gutfeld, for having me on Fox's *Red Eye*. You make me laugh, although I'd like you so much more if you were slightly taller. Bill Schulz and Andy Levy, for shish kebabbing me with your penises. And all of the *Red Eye* behind-the-scenes people and producers for always making me feel welcome.

Colin Quinn, for being a perfect example of exactly what to do, and exactly what not to do in life.

Rachel-Hip Flores, you did an excellent job of researching for me. If only you were able to punch up my shitty jokes.

Bob Kelly Duuuuuude, for convincing me to get an iPhone, thereby contributing to this book. Keith Robinson, Patrice Oneal, and Rich Vos, three of the smartest dummies I know. The *Opie & Anthony* crew, including all of our interns and fifty producers (Steve Carlesi, Stuntbrain, Roland, Derek, Travis, Danny, Sam, E-Rock, Keith the Cop, Mike Cole, Jack, Creampie Jones, British Bob, Duffy's shit teeth, Hip Hop Ron, Tony, and all of you other fuckers whose names I can't remember. My apologies). Ron & Fez and their staff, as well as everyone at CBS Radio and XM Satellite Radio (Sirius XM now, but I'm not convinced I'm not getting fired yet. So I don't want to thank them prematurely and look retarded). Jules Herbert at Barnes & Noble, Zan Farr at Borders, Jill Nicolini and the CW11 for my homoerotic birthday gift, Lynsi S. and the

Acknowledgments

motherfuckin' Philly crew, Gorilla Hisenaj, No Filter Paul and Denise, Master Po, Mars, Don Wickland, and of course, the already-missed Eric Logan. The Comedy Cellar, Caroline's on Broadway, Vinny & Vicky Brand at The Stress Factory, and The Improvs all over the country. Jim Florentine, Don Jamieson, Eddie Trunk, Bobby Levy, Otto Petersen, Kim Hannwacker, Marina Franklin, Al Jackson, Jeff Ross, Greg Fitzsimmons, Dr. Steve for the dick pills, Bob Saget, and Michelle Arnold. Suzanne I. and Beverly L. for all of the help, Joey Silvera, Yoshi, Chelsea Peretti, and Kevin Chiaramonte. Also Kurt Metzger and Mike Morse. Live Nation, especially Jeff Gordon and Geoff Wills, for being consistently good to me. Chris Rock, Sherrod Small, Arde Fuqua, Carolyn Strauss, Pugs & Kelly, Sara and No-Name, Fernando & Greg, Pittsburgh's Jim and Randy, Mike Gallagher, Shred and Regan, The Sports Junkies, BJ Shea and the crew in Seattle, Johnny Darc and Steve Dahl, thanks so much for helping me sell my mediocrity all over the country.

Doug Herzog, Elizabeth Porter, and everyone at Comedy Central, thanks for *Live at Gotham, The Gong Show,* and the *Bob Saget Roast.*

Dave Attell, for not only having me on your show for two episodes, but for being even more uncomfortable in a suit than I am.

Kevin Smith, you're a man of your word, sir. Thanks for putting me in *Zack and Miri Make a Porno.* Please don't cut me out.

Louis C.K., whose red hair and freckles have provided me with endless masturbation fodder.

Jay Leno and the entire *Tonight Show* staff, especially Ross, Bob, and John. Please don't leave; you're the only show who likes me.

And, of course, the fans. To the hardcore Pests, and even the casual fans, I obviously owe my success to you supporting me.